# Albert Einstein

## FORGING THE PATH
## OF MODERN PHYSICS

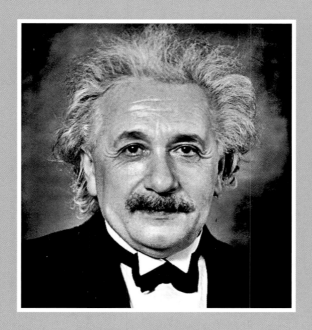

By Diane Dakers

Crabtree Publishing Company

www.crabtreebooks.com

# Crabtree Publishing Company
## www.crabtreebooks.com

**Author:** Diane Dakers
**Publishing plan research and development:**
  Reagan Miller
**Project coordinator:** Mark Sachner,
  Water Buffalo Books
**Editors:** Mark Sachner, Lynn Peppas
**Proofreader:** Wendy Scavuzzo
**Indexer:** Gini Holland
**Editorial director:** Kathy Middleton
**Photo researcher:** Water Buffalo Books
**Designer:** Westgraphix/Tammy West
**Production and print coordinator:** Margaret Amy Salter
**Production:** Kim Richardson
**Prepress technician:** Margaret Amy Salter

Written, developed, and produced by
Water Buffalo Books

**Publisher's note:**
All quotations in this book come from original sources
and contain the spelling and grammatical inconsistencies
of the original text. Some of the quotations may also
contain terms that are no longer in use and may be
considered inappropriate or offensive. The use of such
terms is for the sake of preserving the historical and
literary accuracy of the sources and should not be seen
as encouraging or endorsing the use of such terms today.

**Photographs and reproductions:**
**Alamy:** Keystone Pictures USA: pp. 11, 74, 84; Image
Asset Management Ltd.: p. 16 (left); Everett Collection
Historical: p. 94. **Getty Images:** Mondadori: p. 18
(bottom); Keystone/Hulton Archive: p. 101. **Library of
Congress:** cover (left); pp. 4 (main, right inset), 8, 68,
73, 91 (bottom). **Public domain:** pp. 1, 4 (left inset), 5,
6, 15, 16 (top left, top right), 18 (top), 21 (right), 22, 26,
27, 31, 33, 34, 35, 36, 38, 39, 41, 44 (all), 45, 50, 51, 53, 56,
57, 60, 61, 62 (right), 64 (both), 69, 70, 75 (both), 80, 81,
82, 86 (both), 88, 89, 91 (top), 93, 97, 100, 102, 103 (both).
**Shutterstock:** Anatolii Vasilev: cover (background);
Roman Sakhno: p. 7; Otna Ydur: p. 19 (top); Oleg
Golovnev: p. 28; Nikitina Olga: p. 48; HelgaLin: p.
54. **Wikipedia Creative Commons:** p. 19 (middle);
Bernard Gagnon: p. 10; Mirokado: p. 17; decltype: p.
19 (bottom); GFDL: p. 20; Luidger: p. 21 (top); LoLo00:
p. 25; Rainer Zenz: p. 39; Aliman5040: p. 42 (top); Gerd
Kortemeyer: p. 42 (bottom); Peter Frank, Österreich:
p. 46; che: p. 55; Lou Shornick: p. 83; Ekem: p. 98 (top);
G0T0: p. 98 (bottom); Christopher Michel: p. 99.

**Cover:** A photo of Albert Einstein, the greatest scientific
mind of the 20th and possibly any other century, taken
around 1947, when he was about 68 years old. From
subatomic particles to the relationships between space,
time, matter, and energy, Einstein redefined forever our
understanding of physics and the nature of the universe.

**Library and Archives Canada Cataloguing in Publication**

Dakers, Diane, author
      Albert Einstein : forging the path of modern physics / Diane
Dakers.

(Crabtree groundbreaker biographies)
Includes index.
Issued in print and electronic formats.
ISBN 978-0-7787-1188-9 (bound).--ISBN 978-0-7787-1190-2 (pbk.).--
ISBN 978-1-4271-8937-0 (pdf).--ISBN 978-1-4271-8935-6 (html)

      1. Einstein, Albert, 1879-1955--Juvenile literature. 2. Physicists
--Biography--Juvenile literature. I. Title. II. Series: Crabtree
groundbreaker biographies

QC16.E5D35 2014          j530.092          C2013-907569-0
                                           C2013-907570-4

**Library of Congress Cataloging-in-Publication Data**

Dakers, Diane, author.
  Albert Einstein : forging the path of modern physics / Diane
Dakers.
       pages cm. -- (Crabtree Groundbreaker biographies)
  Audience: Ages 10-13.
  Audience: Grades 7 to 8.
  Includes index.
  ISBN 978-0-7787-1188-9 (reinforced library binding) -- ISBN 978-
0-7787-1190-2 (pbk.) -- ISBN 978-1-4271-8937-0 (electronic pdf)
-- ISBN 978-1-4271-8935-6 (electronic html)
  1. Einstein, Albert, 1879-1955--Juvenile literature. 2. Physicists-
-Biography--Juvenile literature. I. Title. II. Series: Crabtree
groundbreaker biographies.

QC16.E5D355 2014
530.092--dc23
                                           2013043387

# Crabtree Publishing Company
www.crabtreebooks.com          1-800-387-7650

Printed in Canada/012014/BF20131120

**Published
in Canada**
**Crabtree Publishing**
616 Welland Ave.
St. Catharines, Ontario
L2M 5V6

**Published in
the United States**
**Crabtree Publishing**
PMB 59051
350 Fifth Ave., 59th Floor
New York, NY 10118

**Published in the
United Kingdom**
**Crabtree Publishing**
Maritime House
Basin Road North, Hove
BN41 1WR

**Published
in Australia**
**Crabtree Publishing**
3 Charles Street
Coburg North
VIC, 3058

**Chapter 4**  Einstein = "Poet in Science" ....................... 53

**Chapter 5**  Einstein = "The World's Smartest Man" .. 73

**Chapter 6**  Einstein = "Genius" .................................... 91

**Chronology** .............................................................. 104

**Glossary** .................................................................. 106

**Further Information** ................................................ 108

**Index** ....................................................................... 110

**About the Author** .................................................... 112

# Chapter 1
# Going Where Others Had Never Gone

When most boys are 16 years old, their minds are occupied with sports, their schoolmates, and girls. In 1895, when Albert Einstein was that age, his mind was consumed with science.

## Albert Sees the Light

After spending his early years struggling in schools that focused more on memorizing facts than on coming up with original ideas, Albert had finally landed in his ideal educational setting. He spent a year at a high school in Switzerland where teachers encouraged the teen to think for himself. They invited him to ask questions and to focus on his favorite subject—physics. Fueled by this open-minded atmosphere, young Albert's brain turned to the questions that would lead him to become one the greatest physicists of all times.

Albert was particularly fascinated by the nature of light. One day, as he watched sunlight

*Opposite: Three views of Albert Einstein at different stages of his life. Left inset: Albert in 1893 as a young boy of around 14, in Germany. Main photo: between 1921 and 1923, in his early to mid-40s, in Washington, DC; right inset: in 1947, at around the age of 68, probably taken in Princeton, New Jersey.*

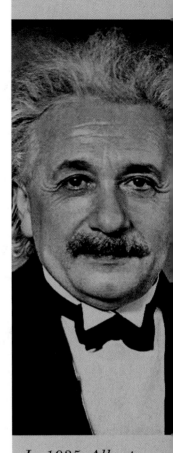

*In 1935, Albert Einstein sat for this formal portrait, taken at the start of his career at the Institute of Advanced Study at Princeton University. At the time, he was about 56 years old.*

dancing on the water, his inquiring mind drifted off in a new and curious direction. The teenager wondered,

*"What would it be like to ride a beam of light? What if one were to run after a ray of light? … If one were to run fast enough, would [the light beam] no longer move at all?"*

This line of questioning, what Albert called his first "thought experiment," consumed the young scientist for years. As it turned out, these teenage musings marked the beginning of what was to become Albert's greatest contribution to the world of physics.

For a decade, Albert pondered his questions about light. He never worked in a laboratory. His only tools were a pencil and paper, and his great brain. Finally, in 1905, when he was 26 years old, the solution to his light-beam puzzle suddenly became crystal clear in his mind. Albert immediately wrote it all down, along with the mathematical equations that explained his thought process. One of those was the now-famous $E = mc^2$. A few months later, a leading German scientific journal published Albert's revolutionary findings, which came to be called the theory of relativity. To Albert, this theory was "beautiful beyond comparison."

## How Dare He?

Not everyone agreed with that opinion. In reality, most people didn't even understand Albert's theory, and many who did were

# What Is Physics?

Physics is a branch of science that deals with matter and energy, and the relationships between them. Physicists study such things as space, time, motion, force, light, magnetism, heat, and the movement of atoms and molecules. Albert Einstein was a theoretical physicist, which is a scientist who makes observations about the world, then tries to explain what he or she sees, using the known beliefs concerning physics. In Albert's case, this meant coming up with new principles, or theories, of physics.

*A beautiful display of sunbeams breaking through clouds in the late-afternoon sky. Scenes like this inspired some of Albert Einstein's earliest musings about the workings of light and other properties of physics, such as electricity and magnetism. In the first of these "thought experiments," as he called them, he wondered what it would be like to be able to move as fast as the speed of light.*

skeptical about it, or not convinced it was correct. The theory of relativity challenged principles of physics that had been accepted for centuries. Not only that, but Albert was so young, how dare he suggest he knew something his more experienced colleagues didn't?

In fact, it would be another 14 years until the scientific world caught up with Albert and proved, once and for all, that his theory of relativity was true.

With that proof came worldwide superstardom for the quirky physicist. For the rest of his life, his every action was the subject of media attention. He traveled the world lecturing and teaching. He was showered with honorary degrees from universities around the globe. He was awarded medals from the world's most highly respected scientific societies, such as the Royal Society of London (1925), the German Physical Society (1929), and the Franklin Institute in Philadelphia (1935). When he was in his early 40s, Albert earned the most revered science award of all—the Nobel Prize for Physics.

*This photo shows the German-born Albert Einstein receiving his certificate of citizenship from Judge Phillip Forman in 1940, thereby officially becoming a citizen of the United States.*

*Most people didn't know what Albert's theory of relativity was all about, but they knew it was important.*

## The People's Scientific Genius

It wasn't just the scientific community that adored Albert, though. Every year, he received fan letters by the thousands, birthday cards from complete strangers, and requests for advice from ordinary people. Considered "the world's smartest man," Albert was as famous in his time as popular musicians, Hollywood actors, and professional athletes are today.

Most people didn't know what Albert's theory of relativity was all about, but they knew it was important—and they loved the quirky and humble fellow who had developed it. "'Saintly,' 'noble' and 'lovable' were the words used to describe him by those who knew him even casually," wrote *The New York Times* after Albert's death in 1955. "He radiated humor, warmth and kindliness. He loved jokes and laughed easily."

In short, Albert may have been smarter than most of us but, in many ways, he was just like all of us. He was a figure of contradictions: a man with a crystal-clear mind but disheveled appearance; a serious thinker who loved nothing more than playing with children on the street; a genius who was so absent-minded, he often forgot his house keys or his briefcase. On occasion, he even got lost on his way home, because he was so lost in thought!

## The Genius Lives on

Today, about 60 years after his death, Albert Einstein is just as famous as he was when he was alive. We see his image on T-shirts and posters, his wild hair sticking up and his tongue sticking out. But it is not just this eccentric image that has kept him in the public eye all this time.

A sculpture of Albert Einstein at a museum in Taiwan. The sculpture captures some of the renowned physicist's most recognizable features—his long unkempt hair, bushy mustache, and rumpled comfortable appearance, that have long endeared him to millions around the globe.

# EINSTEIN, POP CULTURE ICON

On March 14, 1951, tired of being asked to smile for "just one more" picture on the occasion of his 72nd birthday, Albert Einstein responded by sticking his tongue out. Photographer Arthur Sasse captured the shot. After some debate, Sasse's editors decided it would be okay to make the photo public, and it was distributed around the world.

The image became one of the most popular and recognizable photos of the physicist who had once been called "the world's smartest man." Over the years, it has become a part of popular culture, appearing on countless T-shirts, posters, coffee mugs, greeting cards, and other merchandise, including postage stamps! Albert reportedly enjoyed the photo so much that he ordered nine prints for himself, one of which he signed for a reporter. On June 19, 2009, that original signed photo was sold for $74,324. It was a record price for a photo of Albert Einstein.

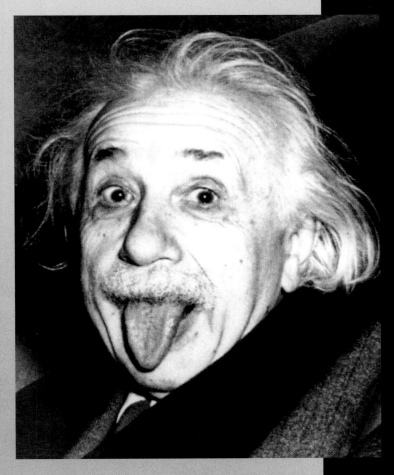

In this electronic age, we owe much to Albert and his progressive thinking. His work has led to computers, cell phones, barcode scanners, and TV remote controls. We have him to thank for fiber optics, x-rays, and laser surgery. Space travel and the Big Bang theory, which explains the formation of the universe, also have their roots in Albert's thought experiments.

"It's not that I'm so smart," he once said about his scientific discoveries, "it's just that I stay with problems longer." Albert believed the keys to his success were stubbornness, curiosity, and an imagination that drove him to "think outside the box," as we would say today.

What makes this classic absent-minded professor even more inspiring is that, in addition to his great brain, Albert Einstein had a great heart. He was a humanitarian who fearlessly spoke out against social ills and injustices wherever he came across them, be it the evil Nazi Party in his homeland of Germany, or racial inequality in his adopted country the United States. He was threatened, criticized, and investigated because of his outspokenness, but he never backed down.

*He was a quiet child who wanted to play alone, a nerdy kid obsessed with science and math, and an excellent student who rebelled against his teachers.*

In 1999, *Time* magazine named Albert Einstein "Person of the Century." The same year, a group of international scientists named him "the greatest physicist ever" and, in a 1999 U.S. poll, Albert came in as the fourth "Most Admired Person" of the 20th century (after Mother Teresa, Martin Luther King Jr., and John F. Kennedy).

Through hard work, creative thinking, and what he called "an irresistible longing to understand the secrets of nature," Albert Einstein forever changed our understanding of the world.

Even as a child growing up in Germany, Albert stood out. He was different than most kids his age—but not necessarily in what people considered a good way. He was a quiet child who wanted to play alone, a nerdy kid obsessed with science and math, and an excellent student who rebelled against his teachers. Even as a little kid, Albert Einstein just wanted to be left alone to do what he did best—to think.

*"I think it was this talent of his to retain the child within himself that aided him in his scientific pursuits. He never lost his childlike awe of the universe, nor did he feel restricted by having to behave like an adult. He could let his mind range freely and sometimes ask preposterous-seeming questions, which ultimately led to elegant answers."*

Evelyn Einstein,
Albert's granddaughter, 2005

# Chapter 2
# Einstein = *Biedermeier,* or "Nerd"

*This photo, taken in Germany in 1893, shows Albert at around the age of 14, about a year before his family moved from Munich, Germany, to Italy.*

**B**orn on March 14, 1879, Albert Einstein was the first child of Hermann and Pauline, a middle-class Jewish couple who lived in the small city of Ulm in the south of Germany. At the time, Hermann sold feather beds for a living. When Albert was 15 months old, Hermann moved the family to the bustling city of Munich, about 100 miles (161 kilometers) to the southeast. There, Hermann and his brother Jakob founded an electrical engineering and manufacturing company called Einstein & Cie.

## Quiet Childhood

From the beginning, Albert was an independent child, happily playing by himself for hours. His sister Maria, whom the family called "Maja," was born when Albert was about two-and-a-half. Despite the occasional temper tantrums directed at his little sister, Albert considered Maja his best friend. This was a relationship that lasted for the rest of their lives. In later years, Maja remembered her brother playing with blocks and building giant houses of cards. Once, the house of cards reached 14 stories

*Albert Einstein's parents, Hermann (photographed around 1890) and Pauline (in the 1870s). Hermann had shown a talent for mathematics when he was in high school, but his parents could not afford to send him to a university to study it further. Albert described his father as "exceedingly friendly, mild, and wise." Pauline came from a well-off family in Ulm, Germany. She loved music and literature.*

*What is believed to be the oldest known photo of Albert Einstein, taken in 1882, when he was around three years old.*

high! She also remembered him throwing things at her when he got angry with her. "It takes a sound skull to be the sister of an intellectual," she joked.

Albert was an unusually quiet child, barely saying a word until long past the age when most children start talking. "My parents were worried because I started to talk comparatively late, and they consulted a doctor because of it," said Albert many years later. When the boy finally started speaking at age three, he didn't just utter a few words—he spoke in full sentences! For the next four years, he remained a reluctant speaker, practicing sentences quietly to himself before saying them out loud. Because of this habit, he was often slow to speak. This behavior led some people, including Albert's teachers when he started school,

# THE HOUSE WHERE ALBERT LIVED

Albert Einstein was not born in a hospital. He was born in his parent's home in Ulm, Germany, a city on the famous Danube River. In World War II, the former Einstein home, which had been built in 1871, was destroyed during an air raid. In one night, on December 17, 1944, bombs destroyed almost 13,000 buildings in the city center, leaving 25,000 people—about three-quarters of the population—homeless.

*Paved over after World War II, the site of Albert Einstein's birthplace in Ulm, Germany, was dug up in 2012 as part of the building of a new train station. This photo shows the exposed cellar. In the background, visible just behind the person pushing a baby stroller, is a memorial marking the site of the house.*

*An undated photo of Albert and his sister Maja.*

*A portrait photo taken of Albert Einstein's younger sister Maja in 1900, when she was around 19 years old.*

to believe he was not intelligent. Little did they know!

Hermann and Pauline raised their children to be independent, curious, well-rounded individuals. A talented piano player, Pauline passed on her love of music to the youngsters. When Albert was five, his mother insisted he learn to play the violin. He nicknamed his violin "Lina." At first, he hated to practice. But, when he was 13, he changed his tune. That's when he discovered a composer named Mozart.

For years, scholars have studied what some researchers have called the "mystic connection" between music and mathematics. It has been said that music is based on logical, mathematical relationships between the notes. Many scholars have therefore focused their research on Mozart because his music is symmetrical, with predictable repeating patterns. Because similar patterns are basic to mathematics, some scholars have even

*Math and music—could they be cousins?
Above: A student works on a mathematical
equation. Right: sheet music from one
of Mozart's compositions. Below right: a
chalkboard used by Albert Einstein at
a lecture he gave in 1931. The last three
lines give numbers that calculate the
density, size, and age of the universe.
Scholars have explored the possibility that
the relationships between notes in music
have some similarities with the logical
relationships in a mathematical equation.
This has led some, including Einstein, to
feel that the music of Mozart and other
gifted composers may be a reflection of
mathematical principles in the universe.*

wondered if Mozart used mathematical
formulas to compose his tunes.

The works and harmonies of this 18th-
century musician so inspired Albert that he
developed a passion for music that would stay
with him for the rest of his life. "Mozart's
music is so pure and beautiful that I see it as

a reflection of the inner beauty of the universe itself," he once said.

The same year he started playing violin, Albert's scientific curiosity made its first appearance. One day when the little boy was sick in bed, Hermann gave him a compass to play with. The device fascinated the child. No matter where he placed it, or how he moved it, the needle always pointed in the same direction. He realized there was some invisible force at work, something he wanted to understand. Why did the compass needle always point north? Years later, Albert recalled this moment. "[The] experience made a deep and lasting impression on me," he said, adding that it made him see that "There must be something deeply hidden behind everything." He spent the rest of his life seeking to understand such "deeply hidden" things.

## Albert + School = Boredom

When he started school at age six, Albert was the only Jew in the Catholic school he attended. His parents chose that school because they weren't particularly religious, and it was less expensive and closer to their home than the Jewish school. Albert felt like an outsider there, partly because of his religion, but mostly because of what other kids and the teachers saw as his odd behavior.

*The Theatine Catholic Church, in Munich, Germany. Munich, the city where Albert Einstein spent most of his youth, is the capital of Bavaria—a predominantly Catholic state. The name of Munich comes from an old German term meaning "by the monks' place." This is a reference to a group of Catholics who founded the city. As a young Jewish boy and an independent-minded student, Albert felt restless and frustrated by the strict discipline imposed by the Catholic school he attended for several years.*

*He loved [mathematics and science] so much that he began to study them on his own at home when he was ten.*

He was quiet, a loner with few friends. He didn't like sports, rough games, or playing soldier—a popular pastime of the day. He asked questions, rather than memorizing and reciting the facts and figures the teachers presented. He rejected the school's strict approach to learning. He also disapproved of the harsh discipline teachers were allowed to dish out to students. Still, Albert got good grades, often ranking at the top of his class.

After only three years at the primary school, Albert was accepted into the Luitpold-Gymnasium. This was a more competitive institution, similar to a middle school or high school, that prepared students for college. He found it even more rigid and stifling than his first school had been. His teachers placed no value on creativity, imagination, or ideas. They did not allow discussion or debate. There were too many rules. Albert's fellow students called him *Biedermeier*, the equivalent of today's "nerd." His teachers called him a "dreamer" because he was always thinking his own thoughts. One teacher even announced to the class that Albert would never amount to anything.

As if to prove the teacher wrong, Albert continued to excel in his classes, even though he didn't put much energy into subjects that bored him. He did not like languages, other than Latin, and hated memorizing dates, names, and places for history class.

Two subjects that didn't bore him were mathematics and science. He loved them so much that he began to study them on his own at home when he was ten. His Uncle Jakob, an engineer and inventor, introduced him to algebra, and a

# LEARN TO LOVE MATH!

Albert Einstein loved mathematics, and you can, too! Here are some of the common branches of the field:

In ALGEBRA, letters such as $x$ and $y$ represent unknown numbers in equations. These letters help us figure out relationships between numbers on opposite sides of the equal sign.

For example, $x + 3 = 5$ is an algebraic equation, or puzzle, where the goal is to figure out that $x = 2$.

GEOMETRY is a branch of mathematics that deals with points in space, lines, curves, angles, three-dimensional shapes, and surface area.

For example, using a geometrical equation, we could figure out how much space (or volume) a square box would take up in a closet. Then we could calculate how many boxes we could fit in that closet!

CALCULUS is a type of math that helps us figure out how much something changes over time, when some of the elements in question also change.

For example, if you are in a car driving steadily at about 50 miles per hour (80.5 km/hr), you would use algebra to figure out how far that car traveled in four hours: $y = 4$ x $50 = 200$ miles (4 x 80.5 = 322 km).

But what if the car's speed changed? If the car accelerated many times during that four hours, the distance it traveled would be more than 200 miles (322 km). You would use calculus to figure out the distance traveled, depending on the rate of acceleration.

family friend, a poor Jewish medical student from Poland named Max Talmud, brought him science, math, and philosophy books. One of Albert's favorites was a multi-volume set, called *Scientific Popular Books*, "a work which I read with breathless excitement," he said.

Before long, Albert's knowledge and understanding were far beyond anything he could learn at school.

## Genius Unleashed

One summer, when Albert was 12, his parents bought him a copy of the geometry book his class was to study during the following school year. Within a few months, he'd worked through all the problems in the book, which he later called his "holy geometry book." He shared his learning with Max, his friend and unofficial tutor and, by the end of the summer, Albert had moved on to calculus and other higher forms of mathematics. "Soon, the flight of his mathematical genius was so high that I could no longer follow," said Max.

When Albert was 15, his life took a dramatic turn. Because of competition from bigger, more successful businesses, the electrical supply company run by his father and Uncle Jakob fell on hard times. The brothers could not earn enough money to keep operating in Germany. A family friend was willing to help them out—if they moved the company to Italy. With financial help from Albert's mother's well-to-do family, the Einstein brothers set up shop first in Milan, Italy, then moved to nearby Pavia.

Hermann and Pauline decided, though, that Albert should stay in Germany to finish his education. The teenager hated the idea, and he lasted just six months without his family. In December of 1894, he left Munich and arrived

*A view of Piazza della Vittoria ("Victory Square," known in the 1800s as Piazza Grande, or "Large Square"), in Pavia, Italy. Shortly after moving to Milan from their native Germany in 1894, the Einstein family pulled up roots again and moved to nearby Pavia, which is shown here at sunset.*

unannounced in Italy, to the surprise of his mom and dad. Because they had raised Albert to be independent, to think for himself, and to make his own choices, his parents accepted his decision to leave the school in Munich. He promised he would continue his education—just not in Germany.

Another reason Albert wanted to leave his native land was that the country required every boy, when he turned 17, to join the army. This was called "mandatory military service," and it was the last thing Albert wanted to do.

# EINSTEIN MYTH #1:
# EINSTEIN FAILED MATH

To encourage kids who struggle in math, it has been reported over and over again that the world's best-known genius, Albert Einstein, failed math class when he was a boy. Not true! In 1935, a friend showed Einstein a headline from a "Ripley's Believe It or Not!" newspaper column that said: "Greatest living mathematician failed in mathematics." When he read this, Albert just laughed. "I never failed in mathematics," he said. "Before I was 15, I had mastered differential and integral calculus." In fact, math was always one of his best subjects at school.

*This document shows Albert Einstein's successful completion of his course of study at the high school he attended in Aarau, Switzerland. The certificate, issued to Albert at the age of 17 in 1896, shows his grades on a number of subjects. On a scale of 1 to 6, with 6 being the highest grade possible, the following scores put to rest the myth that he did poorly in math or math-related subjects: algebra (6), geometry (6), descriptive geometry (6), physics (6), and chemistry (5).*

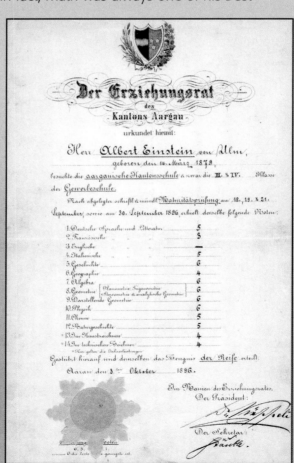

He detested war, guns, and anything to do with the armed forces. In fact, by this time, he had developed such distaste for his homeland in general that, with his father's help (because Albert was underage), he renounced, or gave up, his German citizenship. "The over-emphasized military mentality in the German State was alien to me even as a boy," he said later.

On the other hand, Albert loved Italy, calling the people "the most civilized I have ever met." During the spring and summer of 1895, he passed his time hiking through the Italian countryside, helping out at his father's business and, as he'd promised his parents, studying.

## Going His Own Way

While Hermann wanted his son to take a practical career path into engineering, Albert had a different idea. He wanted a career in science. His goal was to study at the highly regarded Swiss Federal Polytechnic ("the Polytechnic") in Zurich, Switzerland. That fall, he took the entrance exams, confident he would be accepted, despite the fact that he was two years younger than the rest of the applicants.

In October, he was disappointed to learn he had not been accepted into the respected institution—his history and language scores were too low. Still, it was not all bad news. Albert's test scores in science and math had been so exceptional that they caught the attention of the school's director. He suggested the 16-year-old spend a year in the Swiss education system and reapply to the Polytechnic a year later.

On the director's advice, Albert spent a year

*"I have no special talents.
I am only passionately curious."*

at a high school in the nearby town of Aarau, Switzerland. There, he experienced a positive educational environment where teachers welcomed his ideas and questioning ways. As he said later,

*"This school made an unforgettable impression on me thanks to its liberal spirit and the simple earnestness of the teachers, who based themselves on no external authority."*

Albert thrived in this progressive setting. While his Munich classmates had called him "Biedermeier," his fellow students in Aarau described him as "sure of himself," and "unhampered by convention." One called him "a laughing philosopher." Albert was popular with the other kids, and became

more confident in social situations. He played his violin for his new friends, and engaged in lively political discussions.

At the same time, his love of physics flourished and he became intrigued by light. Stimulated by the open-minded atmosphere at school, Albert allowed his thoughts on the subject to wander. It was during this time of his young life that he began wondering what it would be like to ride on a beam of light and whether, if a person could move as fast as the speed of light, the light beam would appear to be standing still.

These questions were the subject of Albert's first-ever scientific paper, "The Investigation of the State of Ether in a Magnetic Field," which he wrote in 1895, at the age of 16. They also formed the basis of what he called his first "thought experiment." Rather than working in a laboratory to find answers to questions, he visualized problems, and came up with solutions, inside his head. This, his first thought experiment, would roll around in his head for 10 years before he came up with the solution he was seeking, the solution that made him famous.

## PICTURE THIS

Albert Einstein not only came up with extraordinary thoughts, but he had a remarkable understanding of the process of his thinking. He once described how he formed and expressed his thoughts as follows: "I very rarely think in words at all. A thought comes, and I may try to express it in words afterwards."

# Chapter 3
# Einstein = (E = mc²)

After failing in his first attempt at admission to the Zurich Polytechnic, Albert Einstein took the entrance exams again a year later. By this time, thanks to his year at the high school in Aarau, he had gained confidence, and his grades in subjects he'd struggled with in the past had improved. French remained his poorest subject. In fact, he barely passed the French portion of the Polytechnic entrance exams the second time around—but pass he did. Albert was accepted into the respected school!

## Albert Goes to College

In the summer before Albert began his studies at the Zurich Polytechnic, the electric company run by his father and uncle in Italy went bust. Uncle Jakob gave up on self-employment and took an engineering job with a more successful company. Hermann, on the other hand, despite his lack of business know-how, started up yet another small business.

That meant the family was, once again, struggling financially. For Albert, it meant his parents could not afford to pay his tuition to the Polytechnic.

*This photo, taken in 1904 or 1905, shows Albert at his job with the patent office in Bern, Switzerland, at around the age of 25 or 26.*

Hermann tried to convince his son to go into engineering and help out in the family business, but Albert was clear on his career goals. He was going to study physics at the Zurich Polytechnic, so he could become a teacher. Fortunately, his mother's wealthy relatives agreed to help the teenager. They covered his tuition at the Swiss school, paid for the room where he lived in Zurich, and gave him a monthly allowance for food and other necessities.

At 17, Albert was the youngest student in his classes at the technical college. He was one of 11 students who started that year in a program designed to train teachers specializing in mathematics and physics. The Polytechnic was much more rigid in its approach to education than the high school in Aarau had been, and it wasn't long before Albert returned to his old ways. He was soon bored by his classes. He thought the professors focused too much on past research, rather than allowing students to explore current theories and develop new ideas of their own. He considered math a waste of his time, and unnecessary to his future in physics.

Later in his life, Albert acknowledged this mistake, and he often consulted with mathematician friends to help him solve his physics problems.

## Early Attitude

Albert never tried to hide his disdain, or disregard, for his teachers. In one lab session, he threw out the professor's notes right in front of him! The trashed documents had outlined the steps for the day's experiment, but Albert wanted to conduct the experiment in his own way.

# EINSTEIN MYTH #2: ALBERT EINSTEIN WAS LEFT-HANDED

For some reason, people have been fascinated by Albert's handedness—was he left-handed or right-handed? As an adult, all photographs show him writing with his right hand, playing violin as a right-hander would, and holding his pipe in his right hand. Strangely, though, the myth that he was left-handed persists. It is possible that he was left-handed as a child, and forced to become right-handed, as was customary in some schools in times gone by. There is little evidence of his early life, photographic or otherwise, to confirm this theory.

*As Albert Einstein's fame grew, people became increasingly starved for details of his life and habits. As a result, numerous stories and myths about him sprang up in the media, making him as much a legendary figure as a brilliant but rather humble physicist. One of these myths had to do with his supposedly being left-handed. This photo, taken at a lecture in Vienna, Austria, in 1921, clearly shows Albert holding a piece of chalk in his right hand.*

In the end, he caused an explosion in the lab, and he had to go to the hospital to get stitches in his right hand. He couldn't write or play the violin for weeks.

During his second year at the Polytechnic, Albert skipped more classes than he attended. He studied on his own, exploring new theories that fascinated him. He took up sailing in nearby lakes, hiked in the countryside, and hung out with friends at cafés in Zurich. There, he smoked a pipe, sipped coffee, and discussed new ideas with his classmates. One of the great friends he met during this time was a math student named Marcel Grossmann, who predicted that "this Einstein will one day be a great man."

Luckily for Albert, Marcel was a dedicated student. Unlike future physicist Albert Einstein, Marcel attended classes and took excellent notes. Come exam time, Albert realized that if he hoped to catch up on everything he'd missed during the past year, he needed those notes. He crammed for weeks before his final second-year exams. Thanks to Marcel, Albert ended up with the highest marks in the class. Marcel came in second.

Albert's academic standing slipped during his third and fourth years at the Zurich Polytechnic. His scorn for his professors grew— and vice versa. Albert felt restricted by their teaching methods and what he perceived as the instructors' lack of knowledge. He thought many of the classes were "useless." At the same time, the teachers were fed up with Albert's disrespect for the institution. One instructor gave him the only failing grade he'd ever earned in physics, saying Albert was "enthusiastic but hopeless at physics." Another called Albert a "lazy dog." Even his relationship with the one instructor he'd initially liked and respected fell apart.

## ALBERT'S BEST FRIEND

Albert Einstein's lifelong good friend Marcel Grossmann was born and raised in Budapest, Hungary. When Marcel was 15, his father, who ran a textile business, moved the family to Switzerland. Marcel met Albert when the two became classmates at the Zurich Polytechnic in 1896. The study notes Marcel famously loaned to Albert survive today, and it is easy to see how the high quality of the notes helped Albert pass his exams.

After graduating from the Polytechnic, Marcel became an assistant to one of his former geometry professors while earning his Ph.D., or doctorate degree.

For the rest of his career, he researched and taught geometry at various colleges in Switzerland.

In 1905, Albert dedicated his doctoral thesis to Marcel. The two men worked together on the general theory of relativity in 1913, with Albert focusing on the physics side and Marcel working on the mathematics side of the theory. A year later, they published another academic paper together. The two remained close friends until Marcel died of multiple sclerosis in 1936 at the age of 58.

*Albert's girlfriend and fellow Zurich Polytechnic student Mileva Maric. A year after failing her final exams at the Polytechnic, Mileva tried again. She retook the exams in July 1901. After she failed for the second time, she knew her dreams of becoming a scientific scholar would never come true.*

By the end of his fourth year, Albert found himself ranked fourth out of five students in his class. He graduated, but barely. The only person who got lower grades than he did was his girlfriend Mileva Maric, who failed to graduate.

## The Science of Romance

Albert Einstein met Mileva Maric, the only female student in his class, in his early days at the Zurich Polytechnic. Mileva was three years older than Albert. She came from a well-off Serbian family, headed by a father dedicated to seeing his daughter succeed. She was brilliant, always at the top of her class, and her dad recognized she could do well in the "man's world" of science and math. He knew she shouldn't be kept from a good education just because she was a girl. Mileva's father insisted his daughter be allowed to study at a first-rate, all-male high school in the city of Zagreb, about 250 miles (402 km) west of the family's hometown. She graduated with the highest marks in her class in physics and mathematics, then made her way to the Polytechnic, where she met Albert.

Born with a hip deformity, Mileva was shy and self-conscious. She was prone to illness and depression, and wasn't considered attractive—physically or in personality. Still, with her great mind and intense nature, Albert was drawn to her. As a piano player and singer, she also shared his love of music. Despite the mutual attraction, it was almost a year after they had become classmates that they had their first date—a day of hiking during the summer of 1897.

The couple's relationship—a blend of science and romance—bloomed over the next three years. During school vacations, when they were apart, they wrote letters to each other. "We understand each other's dark souls so well, and also drinking coffee and eating sausages," Albert once wrote to Mileva. In another letter, he said,

*"When I read Helmholtz [a famous physicist] for the first time, I could not—and still cannot—believe that I was doing so without you sitting next to me. I enjoy working together very much, and I find it soothing and less boring."*

Not a typical love letter!

## Battling Odds

Albert's parents—especially his mother Pauline—objected to their son's relationship with the Serbian girl. They felt she was too old for him, and not pretty enough. She was sickly. She might be smart, but she was clearly not smart enough

to graduate. She was simply not good enough for their boy.

Despite this disapproval, after he graduated from the Polytechnic in 1900, Albert promised he would marry his sweetheart. First, though, he wanted to get a full-time job so he could support her and a family.

As it turned out, this wasn't as easy as he had expected it to be. First of all, to get a job in Switzerland, he had to be a Swiss citizen. Since he had renounced his German citizenship at age 16, he had been stateless, meaning he was not a citizen of any nation. To become a Swiss citizen, he had to prove he was a respectable, hardworking, employable person. He met with the citizenship committee in December 1900 and convinced the group he was worthy.

Albert Einstein became a Swiss citizen in February 1901. But that led to another problem—Switzerland, like his native Germany, had a policy of mandatory military service for its young men. Dutifully, Albert showed up for a medical exam to determine his fitness to serve. Luckily for the war-hating scientist, he had flat

*Albert's first choice in the work world was to find a teaching post, but his lack of enthusiasm for his Polytechnic classes came back to haunt him.*

*This photo of Albert Einstein and Mileva Maric was taken around 1900. This was the year that Albert made up his mind to marry Mileva once he was able to find a job that would provide them with a good living.*

feet and varicose, or swollen, veins in his legs. Because of these ailments, the army rejected him, and he was free to look for work.

## Brilliant Physicist Seeks Employment

Albert's first choice in the work world was to find a teaching post, but his lack of enthusiasm for his Polytechnic classes came back to haunt him. When he went job-hunting, none of his professors would recommend him to potential employers in academia. To survive, he took a series of short-term jobs, working as a private tutor or substitute teacher, until the summer of 1902. In June of that year, he finally landed a permanent position at the Swiss Federal Office for Intellectual Property, commonly known as "the patent office," in Bern, Switzerland.

He got that job thanks to his college chum, Marcel Grossmann. Marcel had heard about an opening for a patent clerk, and had written to Albert to let him know. Marcel's father, a friend of the director of the patent office, recommended Albert for the position. "I would be delighted to get such a nice job, and I would spare no effort to live up to your recommendation," Albert wrote in a letter thanking Mr. Grossmann for his positive reference.

In his post as Technical Expert Third Class, Albert's job was to review new inventions, decide whether they would actually work, and whether they were worthy of a patent. A patent is a legal government document that says the inventor is the only person allowed to make a particular invention. It protects an inventor from someone else stealing his or her discovery. This means that nobody else can manufacture, use, or sell the invention for a given period of time.

*One of the patents Albert Einstein approved was for the mold for Toblerone chocolate bars. Toblerone is known for both its variety of flavor combinations and its unique, pyramid-shaped design.*

As a patent clerk, Albert also helped inventors rewrite complicated patent descriptions to make them more easily understood. He enjoyed the job. He worked six days a week and was remarkably speedy at processing patent applications.

"I was able to do a full day's work in only two or three hours," he said. "The remaining part of the day, I would work out my own ideas." If his boss came along, "I would cram my notes into my desk drawer and pretend to work on my office work." He said it was during this time that "I hatched my most beautiful ideas."

In the evenings and on his days off from the patent office, Albert continued to work on his thought experiments about energy, motion, and the nature of light. He was still looking for answers to his questions about riding on a beam of light.

## Critical Years

Now that he had a full-time job and was financially secure, Albert was ready to marry Mileva. His parents—and hers—still disapproved of the match. Finally, in October 1902, just before he died, Albert's father had a change of heart. He gave his blessing to Albert and Mileva, who married in January 1903. Not a single family member of the bride or the groom came to the wedding. Two friends attended as the only witnesses. Just over a year later, Mileva gave birth to the couple's first son, Hans Albert.

For the next two years, Albert continued to work at the patent office by day. At night, he was consumed with finding solutions to his own

questions about light, time, and motion. He carried a notebook with him wherever he went, even when he was out sailing or taking Hans Albert for a walk, just in case an idea struck him.

He reviewed long-held theories and built on the work of physicists who had come before him, including Isaac Newton, James Clerk Maxwell, and Max Planck. His only tools were his mind and his pencil and paper. He spent so much time thinking and writing notes that he began to neglect Mileva and his son.

*Albert and Mileva lived in an apartment on the second floor of this building in Bern, Switzerland, from 1903 to 1905. This was also the home into which their first son Hans Albert was born in 1904. Today, the building is a museum called Einsteinhaus ("Einstein House"). The museum recreates the Einsteins' second-floor living room, shown here, and houses Albert's biography and life's work on the third floor.*

# The First Baby Einstein

In January of 1902, before they were married, Albert and Mileva had a daughter. They named the baby Lieserl. Because they were living apart at the time of the girl's birth—Albert in Switzerland, and Mileva at her parents' home in Serbia—Albert never met his child. It is believed that he never told anyone, including his parents and sister, about the baby.

In fact, evidence of her existence was not discovered until 1986, more than 80 years after the girl's birth! At that time, researchers found a few references to the baby in a cache, or stash, of never-before-discovered letters.

Other than a few mentions of Lieserl in correspondence between Mileva and Albert, all other evidence of the girl's existence appears to have been deliberately erased. Many scholars have devoted much research to learning the fate of the child. Most believe she was adopted by a friend of Mileva. They also know, because of one cryptic reference in a letter, that the little girl had scarlet fever in September 1903. Some researchers believe Lieserl died of the illness, while others believe she lived with an adopted family, with her identity protected.

In 1905, all of Albert's brainwork paid off. Suddenly, so many ideas filled his head so quickly that he barely had time to write them down. Within eight months, he published four papers in the highly respected German journal *Annalen der Physik* (*Annals of Physics*). With these research papers, Albert changed the world of physics forever.

The research that Albert wrote about in 1905 is among the most significant of the 20th century. It led to discoveries and theories that continue to affect the way we think about physics, as well as the way we live. It will undoubtedly continue to influence the way science affects our lives for generations to come. Albert's research and ideas were also very complex. To this day, even as we benefit from the results of his work, the most

# INSPIRING EINSTEIN 1, 2, & 3

**1** Sir Isaac Newton (1642–1727) (left) was a British physicist, astronomer, mathematician, and philosopher. He laid the foundations for modern physics with his well-known laws of gravity and motion. His theories explained the movement of objects on Earth, as well as that of planets and stars.

**2** Scottish physicist and mathematician James Clerk Maxwell (1831–1879) (below left) brought together a number of ideas about electricity and magnetism. In his work, he proved that if you connect an electric field and a magnetic field, you would get moving waves of energy called electromagnetic waves. He also showed that light is a kind of electromagnetic wave, and he even figured out the speed of light.

**3** German physicist Max Planck (1858–1947) (below, seated center) believed that energy, including light, does not flow in steady waves, but rather, travels as tiny packages of energy, which he called "quanta." (The singular of "quanta" is "quantum.") With his findings, called quantum theory, Planck gave the world of physics a new understanding of the structure of light and radiation. He is shown here with Albert Einstein (second from left) at a gathering of prominent physicists in Berlin, Germany, in 1931.

educated readers continue to struggle to get their minds around much of what Albert wrote!

## The Einstein Papers

Albert's first paper in 1905 focused on the structure of light. For years, some physicists had believed that light travels in waves, while other physicists said it is made up of individual "packets" of light. Each group of physicists thought the other was wrong, but Albert proved that both were correct! In this paper, Albert showed that light travels in waves, but he also showed that those waves are made up of individual packets of particles of light. These packets of light particles are called photons. A photon is a basic building block of light, just as an atom is a basic building block of matter.

Albert also showed that photons could actually blast electrons right out of molecules of metal. This release of electrons was called the photoelectric effect, and it led to a new science called quantum physics. (A quantum is a packet, or quantity, of energy in any

# OLAR) **POWER** OF
# )TOELECTRIC **EFFECT**

st common applications of the photoelectric effect is the
otovoltaic cell. A solar cell converts sunlight into electricity.
ells were built in the 1880s, but the inventors who created
ow exactly how they worked. When Albert Einstein figured
ectric effect in 1905, the inner workings of solar cells finally

e made of thin layers of silicon. When
ight hit a solar cell, some of them are
e cell, and they knock electrons out of
is. Those electrons travel along wires
and create power. Solar cells are used in
ich as watches, radios, and calculators,
io be grouped into large panels to power
ime, or fuel an airplane.

*voltaic cell provides enough*
*) keep this device running well*
*ction as a pocket calculator.*
*the top of the calculator.*

electromagnetic wave. Photon is the name for
a specific quantum, or quantity, of light.) This
science has, in turn, led to many inventions,
including television, lasers, and computer chips.

Albert's second research paper of 1905 proved
that molecules and atoms exist, something
that had long been suspected, but never
confirmed. He said, too, that, by using certain
equations, a scientist could calculate the size
of unimaginably small atoms and molecules.
This paper also explained the effect of fast-
moving atoms and molecules on particles in a

liquid. This effect, called "Brownian motion," was named for Robert Brown (1773–1858), a Scottish botanist, or plant scientist.

*"This had been going around and around at the back of his head for years, and suddenly, [the principle of relativity] wanted to thrust itself forward into his conscious mind."*

One of Albert's greatest insights came to him in the spring of 1905. One day in May, he woke up in the morning with the answer he had been seeking since he was a 16-year-old thinking about

# BROWNIAN MOTION

In 1827, when botanist Robert Brown was examining tiny grains of pollen suspended in water under his microscope, he noticed they were moving around in a wiggling, zigzag pattern. His research showed that this movement wasn't caused by other life forms in the water, but he couldn't explain what he saw. In 1905, Albert Einstein finally explained it, proving the existence of atoms and molecules at the same time.

Albert showed that the pollen moved because it was being bombarded by thousands of water molecules. Because the water molecules are so much tinier than even a single pollen particle, they are invisible, even under a microscope. That's why it looked as if the grains of pollen were moving on their own! Albert also proved that, using certain calculations, a scientist could figure out how many water molecules were hitting a single grain of pollen at a given time, and how fast those water molecules were moving.

# ATOMS: TEENY-TINY BUILDING BLOCKS

Everything in the world is made up of atoms and molecules. Atoms are individual building blocks, and molecules are combinations of those building blocks. The Periodic Table of the Elements lists the 118 known types of atoms. For example, one of those is hydrogen, represented on the Periodic Table as H. Another is oxygen, represented by the letter O. When two hydrogen atoms combine with one oxygen atom, they form a molecule called $H_2O$. That is water.

Each atom is made up of a center, called a nucleus, that contains protons and neutrons. Protons and neutrons are subatomic particles. As "subatomic" suggests, these particles are smaller than atoms. The nucleus is also surrounded by a cloud of subatomic particles called electrons. In his explanation of the "photoelectric effect," Albert Einstein showed that a quantum, or quantity, of light called a photon could cause metal molecules to release electrons. Such discoveries about the structure and make-up of atoms, and how they can be affected by other particles, has opened the door to many amazing discoveries and inventions. These range from nuclear power, to cell phones and the Internet, to new ways of diagnosing and treating cancer and other diseases, to discoveries about how the universe came into being and what we might find as we expand our horizons in outer space.

*This diagram shows the basic structure of an atom. The number and structure of subatomic particles (protons, neutrons, and electrons) are simplified, with circles showing the path of the electrons as they move around the nucleus.*

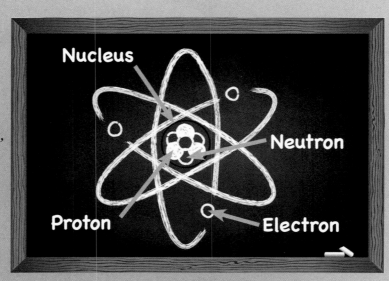

riding on a beam of light. "He suddenly saw the idea," said one of his friends. "This had been going around and around at the back of his head for years, and suddenly, it wanted to thrust itself forward into his conscious mind."

# It's All Relative

Until Albert Einstein and his special theory of relativity came along, physicists believed that time and space were constant. This means that a minute was a minute was a minute, no matter where you were or what you were doing. That also meant that a mile or a kilometer was always the same length, and the mass of an object never changed. They believed the only thing that changed was the speed of light.

Albert realized, though, that it was the other way around: The speed of light was constant, and all the other elements changed depending on how fast the viewer was moving through space.

For example, if you are standing still watching a train zip by, the train appears to be going very quickly. If, however, you are in a car driving beside that train, moving in the same direction, the train would appear to be traveling more slowly. If you are traveling at exactly the same speed as the train, it would look as if the train isn't moving at all. In other words, the apparent speed of the train is related to the motion of the person looking at it. This is, basically, the special theory of relativity.

Albert also believed that, if he could travel at the speed of light by riding on a light beam, *everything* around him would slow down, including time. He proposed that the faster a body can move through space, the more slowly time passes for that person, or object, compared to how fast time passes for someone standing still. That means the wristwatch of someone traveling at the speed of light would actually run more slowly than that of someone at rest.

Confused? So was everyone else—even other physicists—at the time Albert proposed this theory. That's because we can't possibly travel fast enough to notice this effect. We can't travel at the speed of light, so it's almost impossible to imagine this concept. Today, though, scientists rely on Albert's theories when they calculate the possibilities of traveling unimaginable distances in outer space.

Albert called this idea his "principle of relativity," and it was the most groundbreaking, or pioneering, concept the world of physics had ever seen. This theory, which was later renamed the "special theory of relativity," was the topic of the third paper Albert published in the *Annalen der Physik* in 1905. A few weeks later, he sent the journal a fourth paper, a little three-page addendum, or addition, to his special theory of relativity. It contained and explained his famous equation, $E = mc^2$.

In between publishing these four groundbreaking research papers, Albert also earned his Ph.D. from Zurich University in 1905. Given his remarkable contributions to science in such a short period of time, 1905 has been dubbed his *annus mirabilis*, which is Latin for "year of wonders." The work Albert did that year brought him superstardom in the world of physics and led him to achieve his dream of becoming a professor. It would also lead him to receive one of the world's greatest honors—the Nobel Prize in Physics.

*"When a man sits with a pretty girl for an hour, it seems like a minute. But let him sit on a hot stove for a minute— then it's longer than any hour. That's relativity!"*

Albert Einstein

# E = MC² TRANSLATED

$E = mc^2$ (the raised "2" is translated as "squared") is the most famous equation in history. Most people have heard of it, but most of us don't know what it means. Albert Einstein figured out that everything that is made out of atoms and molecules—which is everything in existence—can be converted into energy. He also figured out that the speed of light is the connection between the mass, or weight, of an object and the energy it can produce. In his legendary equation, "E" stands for "energy," "m" stands for the "mass" of the object or atom in question, and "c" represents the speed of light. Using this formula, scientists can tell how much energy an object can produce.

It was 25 years before scientists could begin to prove that this equation was correct. It was that long until they developed the equipment needed to test the theory that Albert had come up with in his head!

Here are a few "molecules" of $E = mc^2$ trivia:
- In the equation, "c" stands for *celeritas,* which is Latin for "speed."
- The speed of light is about 186,282 miles (299,792 km) per second.
- At that speed, you could circle Earth seven and a half times in one second.

*Sailors spell out "E = mc² x 40" on the flight deck of the USS* Enterprise. *The world's first nuclear-powered aircraft carrier, the* Enterprise *first set sail in 1961. It became inactive 40 years later, in 2001, when this photo was taken. Albert Einstein's famous formula helped scientists turn the power of the atom into a source of energy to fuel ships like the* Enterprise. *Many times during the ship's life, sailors spelled out the formula to honor its creator and the role he played in the deployment of their ship.*

# Chapter 4
# Einstein = "Poet in Science"

Today, we know that Albert Einstein was a genius. But, in 1905, not everyone in the world of physics accepted his groundbreaking theories. After all, he was only 26 years old, and he dared challenge scientific principles that had been accepted for hundreds of years. Not only that, but his ideas were so hard to understand that few others could even grasp them at first. Albert had hoped his new notions would catch the attention of universities, and that he would be flooded with job offers. Instead, he ended up working at the patent office for another four years.

## The University Universe

Even though he still didn't have his dream job of teaching physics, Albert did get a bit of good news on the work front. In April 1906, he was promoted to Technical Expert Second Class at the Swiss Patent Office. That meant a higher salary. It also meant he still had lots of time to work on his thought experiments, to continue to come up with new ideas, and to develop new theories of physics. In 1906, he published six scientific papers. In 1907, he published ten more. Other physicists—including the famous Max Planck— started paying attention.

*Albert Einstein at his desk at the University of Berlin, Germany, in 1920.*

*When Albert Einstein wrote his* Annus Mirabilis *("Year of Wonders") papers in 1905, his ideas were so new and difficult to understand that his groundbreaking theories weren't immediately accepted by other scientists. In 1906 and 1907, however, Albert wrote more important papers and he gradually began getting the attention of other physicists. Over the years, his ideas gained great acceptance, and* $E = mc^2$ *would become the most famous equation of all time.*

In 1908, Albert finally got a teaching position, as a sort of private instructor at the University of Bern, in Switzerland. It was a part-time position, and it didn't pay enough that he could quit his job at the patent office. Still, it gave him a foot in the door of academia.

A year later, when Albert was 30 years old, his dream of becoming a university professor came true at last. The University of Zurich hired him to teach physics. This meant he could finally quit his job at the patent office. That same year, in July, he earned an honorary doctorate degree (the first of many) from the University of Geneva. A year later in 1910, he was nominated for, but did not win, the Nobel Prize in Physics for his special theory of relativity.

Around this time, as Albert's commitment to teaching and research was on the rise, his dedication to his family began to diminish. In January 1911, the German University in Prague in Czechoslovakia (now the Czech Republic) offered to double Albert's salary if he would teach there. His wife Mileva wasn't happy with the idea. She liked living in Zurich, and she knew Prague was a city in the throes of conflict because of differing beliefs among its citizens.

Mileva worried her family wouldn't fit in, and might even be unsafe, given the social divide among the German, Czech, and Jewish communities there. Despite his wife's objections, Albert accepted the job, and moved his family to the foreign city, 435 miles (700 km) to the northeast.

In 1911, Albert was a sought-after scientist. He began traveling throughout Europe, attending conferences, and leaving Mileva

*The Rudolfinum, a concert hall that opened in 1885 in Prague, Czechoslovakia (now the Czech Republic). In 1911, against the wishes of his wife Mileva Albert Einstein accepted a university professorship in Prague and moved his family away from Zurich.*

*This photo shows participants at the first Solvay Conference, in 1911. Since then, there have been 24 more Solvay Conferences on physics, and 22 on chemistry. Albert Einstein (shown standing, second from right) and his colleague Marie Curie (seated, second from right) attended many of the early conferences. The gatherings still take place in Brussels, Belgium.*

on her own more and more often. In October 1911, he was one of 20 of the world's most brilliant physicists invited to participate in the invitation-only Solvay Conference in Brussels, Belgium. At 32, he was the youngest participant at the gathering of brains that included such scientific giants as Max Planck. It was at Solvay that Albert met Nobel Prize winner Marie Curie for the first time. The two scientists would become lifelong friends. While the group was in Brussels, Madame Curie, the only woman at the conference, learned that she had been awarded the Nobel Prize for the second time.

# MARIE CURIE

Probably the most famous female scientist of all time, Marie Curie was also a woman of firsts. Born in Poland in 1867, she attended college in Paris, France, where she was one of just 23 women among the 1,825 students in the School of Science. After earning a master's degree in physics and another in mathematics, she focused her research on radioactivity. She even invented the word "radioactivity."

She made history in 1903 when she became the first woman to win the Nobel Prize in Physics. She shared the honor with her husband Pierre, with whom she had made significant breakthroughs in the field of radioactivity.

In 1911, Marie made history again, when she won a second Nobel Prize, this one in Chemistry, for her discovery of two new radioactive elements - Radium and Polonium (named for Poland). She was the first scientist to win two Nobel Prizes. She remains one of just two women who have earned the prestigious prize in physics, and one of four women to win the chemistry prize.

Marie's husband Pierre died in 1906 after being hit by a horse-drawn wagon. Marie died in 1934 of illness related to her exposure to radioactive materials. One of the couple's daughters, Irène, became a chemist and, a year after her mother's death, earned a Nobel Prize in Chemistry.

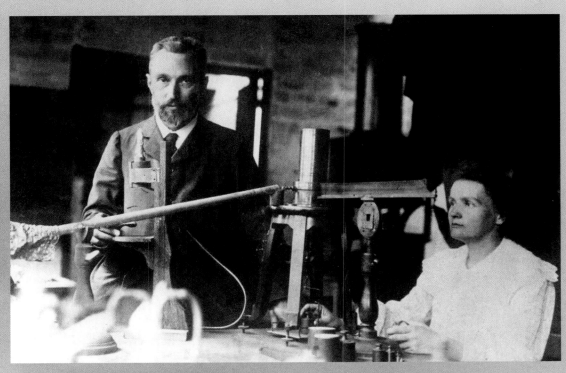

A year later, in 1912, Albert was nominated for the Nobel Prize in Physics for a second time. Again, he did not win. But, by this point in his career, he fully expected he would win the coveted prize one day.

Over the next few years, Albert became more and more in demand by universities across Europe. He was lured away from Prague after just a year to take a post at his *alma mater*, or former school, the Zurich Polytechnic, now called the Swiss Federal Institute of Technology. Albert welcomed the chance to return as a successful physicist to the school where he had once been called a "lazy dog." Mileva was thrilled to return to the Swiss city she loved.

Albert was not a typical university professor. Instead of dressing in a neat suit and tie, he was always rumpled in his baggy pants and ill-fitting jackets. He was disorganized, reading from lecture notes he'd scribbled on scraps of paper. Still, his students loved his good humor and humility, and his friendly open approach to teaching.

After all those years he had dreamed of becoming a professor, what surprised Albert most about teaching was that he didn't like it. It got in the way of his research. So, less than two years later, when the University of Berlin in Germany offered him a non-teaching post as director of a new institute of physics, Albert moved his family again. By this time, though, Mileva—with whom Albert had a second son, Eduard, in 1910—had had enough. She was feeling neglected. She wanted more time with her husband and, as a fellow scientist, wanted to help him with his work. Albert wanted her to stay home with the boys.

For Mileva, the move to Berlin in the spring of 1914 was the last straw. She hated the city and felt "starved for love," complaining that Albert spent more time with science than with his family. Three months after arriving in the German capital, Mileva, Hans Albert, and Eduard boarded a train back to Zurich, never to return. Albert cried for the rest of the day his family left, but he stayed in Berlin. He never lived with his sons again.

## Wartime = Pacifism + Science

In July 1914, about a month after Mileva and the boys left Albert in Berlin, World War I began in Europe. Germany was at the center of the conflict, siding with Austria-Hungary against most of the world's great nations, including the United States, Canada, Britain, and France.

Albert hated war. He was a pacifist, someone who believes that war and violence are morally wrong and should not be used to solve the world's problems. It shocked him to see German citizens lining up to celebrate soldiers marching off to fight. Even more sickening to Albert, though, was the fact that almost 100 leading German scientists signed a document supporting Germany's bullying military tactics. Einstein was one of just three scientists

## ELEMENTS OF EINSTEIN

Albert Einstein was nominated for the Nobel Prize in Physics almost every year between 1910 and 1921. He finally won in 1921 and was awarded the prize in 1922.

who opposed Germany's actions, signing an antiwar "Manifesto to Europeans."

Albert spoke publicly against war and against Germany's pro-war position, taking a stance that would later cause him to fear for his safety in his homeland. He was a crusader for democracy, wrote letters campaigning for peace, and asked awkward questions of government officials. Mostly, though, while World War I raged around him, Albert turned to physics to help him through this time of international upheaval.

Between November 1915 and February 1917, he published 15 scientific papers, including the article that would make him an international celebrity.

Since he'd published his special theory of relativity in 1905, Albert had been troubled by one thing about it—the theory only addressed objects moving at constant motion. It did not take into account acceleration (speeding up) or deceleration (slowling down). As usual, Albert let this problem brew around in his brain until he came up with an idea.

In 1907, out of the blue, he had what he called "the happiest thought of my life." Later, he described the moment:

*"The breakthrough came suddenly one day. I was sitting on a chair in my patent office in Bern. Suddenly the thought struck me: If a man falls freely, he would not feel his own weight. I was taken aback. This simple thought experiment made a deep impression on me."*

He realized that, in this scenario, gravity caused the falling man to accelerate, or speed up, as he got closer to the ground. All the man's molecules accelerated at the same speed, so the man would feel weightless on the way down. Gravity was the accelerating force Albert could use to advance his special theory of relativity!

It would be another eight years before he had it totally figured out, and it was a painstaking process. "Every step is devilishly difficult," he wrote to a friend. He called on his old chum Marcel Grossmann to help him with the mathematics side of the problem. Finally, in 1915, he wrote to his son, Hans Albert, "I have just completed the most splendid work of my life." In March 1916, *Annalen der Physik* published Albert Einstein's most celebrated paper, "The Foundation of the General Theory of Relativity."

## The Proof Is in the Stars

According to the general theory of relativity, everything—including light—is affected by gravity. That means starlight passing by the Sun would be pulled toward the Sun by the Sun's gravity. That, in turn, means the starlight should bend as it passes the Sun. But how could Albert prove this? He may have come up with one of the most radical concepts in the history of physics, but it would take a solar eclipse before astronomers could prove his theory was true.

The only way Albert could think of to confirm his theory was to compare a star's position in the

sky at two different times of year—once when the star appeared close to the Sun, and once when it appeared farther away. When a star is close to the Sun in the sky, though, you can't see it because of the glare from the Sun. Albert realized he needed to wait for a solar eclipse. That way, the sky around the Sun would be dark, and astronomers would be able to see the star. Unfortunately, Albert had a long wait, because the next solar eclipse was three years away.

Finally, the day of the eclipse, May 29, 1919, arrived. Two teams of British astronomers observed and took photographs showing the position of stars during the five minutes the Moon blocked out the Sun that day. One team

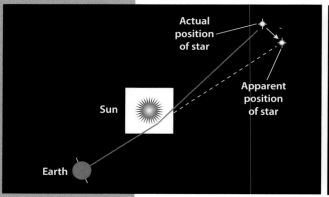
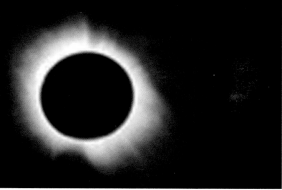

*This diagram illustrates a beam of light from a star passing by the Sun and continuing on to Earth. The Sun's gravity is strong enough to pull the beam of light toward it, curving the beam around the Sun so it is visible from Earth, as shown here. This bending of light around the Sun was demonstrated in the solar eclipse on May 29, 1919, which is shown in the photograph at right. This and other photographs of the sky around the Sun during the eclipse proved Albert Einstein's theory that everything, including light, is affected by gravity.*

conducted observations in Africa, with a second team based in Brazil to double-check the results.

When the astronomers analyzed their data, or information, they discovered Albert was correct—the Sun's gravity had pulled starlight off course, making a star appear to be in a different place than it actually was.

Six months after the eclipse, after astronomers had compiled their data, and the heads of two different British astronomy societies had reviewed it, the Astronomer Royal of England made an announcement: "After careful study of the [photos], I am prepared to say that there can be no doubt that they confirm Einstein's predictions."

*"One thing at least is certain. Light has weight. One thing is certain and the rest debate— Light rays, when near the sun, do not go straight."*

Albert Eddington, the astronomer in charge of the solar eclipse project that proved Albert Einstein's general theory of relativity

Physicists and astronomers celebrated. "This is one of the most important results obtained in connection with the theory of gravitation since Newton's day," said one. "The result is one of the highest achievements of human thought."

It was the first new theory about gravity in 250 years—and it made news around the world. Suddenly, "Albert Einstein" was a household name. Even though most people didn't understand his work, they liked the idea that someone had come up with a whole new view of the universe. It was mysterious and exciting, a

**REVOLUTION IN SCIENCE.**

**NEW THEORY OF THE UNIVERSE.**

**NEWTONIAN IDEAS OVERTHROWN.**

**LIGHTS ALL ASKEW IN THE HEAVENS**

Men of Science More or Less Agog Over Results of Eclipse Observations.

**EINSTEIN THEORY TRIUMPHS**

Stars Not Where They Seemed or Were Calculated to be, but Nobody Need Worry.

*Albert Einstein's general theory of relativity was news all over the world. Shown here: Headlines for a November 6, 1919, story in* The Times *of London (left) and, the next day, a front-page story in* The New York Times. *The* New York Times *story reported that when Albert's theory was accepted for publication, he warned the publishers that no more than 12 people in the world would understand it!*

little taste of science fiction on Earth. The public also liked the fact that German and British scientists had worked together on this project. The two nations had been enemies in World War I, which had ended a year earlier. People all over the world were in the mood for some good news.

## Personal Problems

Things may have been progressing brilliantly in Albert's professional life but, by this time, his personal life was quite unsettled. During the war years, it was difficult to travel in Europe, so Albert rarely saw his sons. He kept in touch with them via letters, but he missed the boys. Eduard was often ill, and a source of constant worry for the scientist.

In 1915, Albert and Mileva started arguing (through their letters) about money, and how their children were to spend vacations. The tone of Hans Albert's letters to his father also began to change. He wrote less and less about his interest in mathematics and learning to play the piano, hobbies he shared with his father. Instead, he wrote about needing money, and not wanting to spend holiday time with his dad. "My fine boy has been alienated from me for a few years already by my wife, who has a vengeful [unforgiving] disposition," Albert wrote to a friend. Later, to the same friend, he wrote: "The boy's soul is being systematically poisoned to make sure that he doesn't trust me."

By the middle of 1916, Albert's conflict with Mileva, and therefore the boys, settled down. Their letters became strained but polite. Over the next three years, until Albert and Mileva finally divorced, their relationship alternated between turmoil and truce.

Part of the problem was that, in 1912, Albert had reconnected with his cousin Elsa during a trip to Berlin. The two had been childhood friends, but had lost touch over the years. Now, Elsa was divorced and living in Berlin with her two daughters. Unlike Mileva, who was gloomy and bitter, Elsa was warm and even-tempered, a personality Albert preferred.

When Albert and Mileva moved to Berlin in 1914, his relationship with Elsa deepened. They became romantically involved. After Mileva and the boys moved away, Elsa took care of Albert in a nurturing and motherly way, cooking for him and nursing him back to health when he was ill.

# COUSINS

...id it. Britain's Queen Victoria and King William III did it, as did ...ime minister Sir John A. Macdonald. The famous British naturalist ...American bank robber Jesse James, and writer Edgar Allan ...the list of people who married their first cousins. While it may ...aboo, or socially unacceptable, to marry your cousin today, it is ...st countries. In fact, the United States is the only country in the ...where marrying your auntie's kid is prohibited—and it's not even ...ate. Only 16 states have out-and-out bans on cousins tying

...t socially unacceptable—to marry your cousin in Canada, Britain, ...some countries around the world, notably in a number of ...nations, it is actually encouraged.

It would be five years before Albert negotiated a divorce with Mileva—partly because he was focused on his general theory of relativity, and partly because he liked living as a bachelor in Berlin. He knew that, as soon as he got a divorce from Mileva, Elsa would want to marry him, and he wasn't ready for that.

Finally, in 1919, Albert and Mileva were divorced. Four months later, he and Elsa got married.

## Albert's Rising Star

Newly married and now a superstar of science thanks to his general theory of relativity, Albert Einstein suddenly found himself in the international spotlight. He gave speeches all over Europe, and was awarded an honorary doctorate from the University of Rostock, Germany, the only such award he would ever earn in his homeland.

Not everyone admired Albert, though. Because he had spoken out against World War I, and because Germany had lost the war, some Germans were suspicious of him. Plus, he was Jewish. During the post-war years, anti-Semitism, or prejudice against Jews, was on the rise in Germany. Albert's reaction to this hatred of Jews was to connect to his Jewish heritage and learn more about his cultural roots.

He joined the Zionist movement, a campaign dedicated to establishing a Jewish homeland in the Middle East. (Israel would become that place in 1948.) Albert believed such a land would provide safety from discrimination for Jews. When Zionist leader Chaim Weizmann invited Albert and Elsa to join him on a speaking tour of the United States, the couple agreed.

On April 2, 1921, Albert and Elsa arrived in America for the first time. When they landed in New York City, thousands of fans turned up at the docks to greet their ship. Over the next

*Albert and his second wife, Elsa, on a ship sailing to the United States in 1921.*

two months, the Einsteins traveled through the northeastern United States. At every stop, Albert spoke about his theories and helped Chaim Weizmann raise money for the Hebrew University of Jerusalem in Palestine (modern-day Israel).

During a visit to Washington, DC, Albert met U.S. president Warren G. Harding. In New York, he reconnected with his tutor from his childhood in Munich. Max Talmud, who now went by the name Max Talmey, had become a successful doctor in New York.

Everywhere he went, Albert was mobbed, "flooded with questions, invitations, and suggestions from admirers," he said. Like many celebrities, Albert had a love-hate relationship with the media attention and his superstar status. On one hand, he said he felt as though he was being "shown around like a prize-winning ox." On the other hand, he was proud to use his fame to raise awareness "for the Jewish cause."

Dubbed the "Poet in Science" by *The New York Times*, Albert wasn't a typical bookish scientist. People loved his gentle manner, the twinkle in his eye, his charming and refreshing nature, and, of course, his wild hair. "Just as with the man in the fairy tale who turned whatever he touched into gold, with me, everything is turned to newspaper clamor," he said.

*Albert and Elsa pose before a group of government buildings on their visit to Washington, DC, during their trip to the United States in 1921.*

*Albert Einstein is shown in New York with Chaim Weizmann (second from right) and other Jewish leaders on a tour to raise money for the Hebrew University of Jerusalem in 1921.*

After his visit to the United States, Albert traveled to Great Britain, Czechoslovakia, Austria, and France. While he and Elsa were in Paris, Albert received death threats because of his scientific views, his political beliefs, and his Jewish heritage.

# ALBERT'S RELIGIOUS ROOTS

When Albert was a child, his family was Jewish, but not particula devoted to the religion. At the time, though, German law require children to learn about whichever faith the family followed, so A studied Judaism with a distant relative until he was 12. At that p passion for science began to conflict with his religious studies. "the reading of popular scientific books, I soon reached the conv that much in the stories of the Bible could not be true," he said. be 30 years before his interest in his Jewish heritage returned.

Albert's life was a whirlwind of travel, speaking engagements, and newspaper interviews. His favorite subjects of discussion were pacifism, peace, freedom, Zionism, and, of course, relativity. His goal was to use his fame to make the world a better place.

Another goal was to win the Nobel Prize in Physics, and he had no doubt he would do so. As far as Albert was concerned, it wasn't a matter of if he was going to win the coveted prize, but when.

## An Unusual Route to the Prize

In the fall of 1921, the Nobel Academy did a bizarre thing. Even though the group had overwhelmingly voted to give the physics award to Albert that year, one particular scientist didn't think he should get it. Rather than give the award to anyone else, the Academy decided to "bank" it until they could sway the negative voter. After all, Albert Einstein was the most famous scientist in the world. How could they give the Nobel Prize in Physics to anyone else?

# Einstein Myth #3: Albert Gave Away His Nobel Prize Money

For more than 80 years, it was believed that Albert Einstein gave Mileva Maric the cash winnings from his 1922 Nobel Prize win. This arrangement was said to have been part of the couple's 1919 divorce agreement. The prize money, approximately $32,000, amounted to more than 10 times the average salary for a university professor at the time. In 2006, newly revealed letters showed that Albert had, in fact, only given Mileva part of his winnings. The rest he invested in U.S. enterprises. He lost most of it during the Great Depression, or economic crash, of the late 1920s and early 1930s.

A year later, in November 1922, after having been nominated—but not winning—on many previous occasions, and having had his award delayed, Albert received official word of his 1921 Nobel victory. That meant he won the 1921 Nobel Prize at the same time his colleague Niels Bohr won the 1922 award. Because Albert and Elsa were in the middle of a trip through Asia at the time, he did not attend the award ceremony in Sweden in December.

In the end, Albert Einstein won the Nobel Prize "for his service, to Theoretical Physics and especially for his discovery of the law of the photoelectric effect"—the subject of one of his 1905 papers. His theory of relativity, still considered too controversial, was never mentioned. Six months after he missed the official ceremony, Albert finally gave his Nobel Lecture in Sweden. The subject of his talk? Relativity.

*"Only two things are infinite—the universe and human stupidity—and I'm not sure about the former."*

Albert Einstein

# Chapter 5
# Einstein = "The World's Smartest Man"

After earning the Nobel Prize for Physics, Albert Einstein was even more in demand, and he became even more famous. He traveled the world lecturing and teaching, but he never lost his passion for problem solving. In the early 1920s, he started along a new line of thought, one that involved finding a connection between electromagnetics, gravity, space, and time. Other scientists thought he was wasting his time, but Albert continued to work on this "unified field theory" for the rest of his life. Meanwhile, his career was about to take him permanently away from Europe and over to the other side of the Atlantic Ocean.

## Back in the U.S.A.
In December 1930, Albert took a short-term post as a visiting professor at the California Institute of Technology ("Caltech") in Pasadena. When he and Elsa arrived in America, Albert was once again the subject of media frenzy. "Swarms of reporters boarded the ship," he said. "An army of photographers... pounced on me like starved wolves."

Despite this, Albert enjoyed Pasadena, with its "sunshine and fresh air, gardens with palm and pepper trees, and friendly people who smile at one and ask for autographs." He ended up returning to the sunny city for two more winters, teaching—and tolerating his newfound celebrity status. Everyone wanted to meet him, including the famous actor Charlie Chaplin!

While Albert enjoyed what he called the "paradise" of California, though, a dark cloud was hovering over his native land. The oppressive Nazi Party was gaining power. Early in 1933, it took over Germany. The party and its leader, Adolf Hitler, hated Jews and wanted to "rid" Germany of them. Because Albert had previously spoken out against Nazis and war, and because he was a Jew, he knew that he and

# ANTI-SEMITISM: A HISTORICAL HATRED

Historically, the term "Semite" has referred to people connected through Semitic languages such as Hebrew, Arabic, and Aramaic. These people have included Arabs, Jews, and others living in present-day Egypt, Lebanon, Syria, Ethiopia, Jordan, and Israel, among other nations. Today, the term "anti-Semitism" refers exclusively to prejudice or hatred against Jews.

Sadly, this hatred is not new to Jews. Some say it actually started in biblical times. We do know that about 2,000 years ago, in the Roman Empire, conflict erupted when Jews refused to worship Roman gods. Before long, Christianity became the official religion of the Roman Empire, and Rome became the seat of the Catholic Church. For centuries, Christians held to the belief that the Jews were collectively responsible for the killing of Jesus. Official decrees from the Church and other forms of discrimination forced Jews in many Christian countries to flee to other parts of the world.

Since the Middle Ages, campaigns designed to get rid of Jews have occurred time and time again. Thousands of Jews have been killed during these times. The most recent mass killing of Jews took place during World War II, when Adolf Hitler, the Nazi Party, and those who aided the Nazis, slaughtered 6 million European Jews on religious as well as racial and ethnic grounds.

*In the 1920s and 1930s, Albert Einstein saw the signs of trouble in Germany that eventually led him to move to the United States. Top: Adolf Hitler (upper left corner of photo) gives the Nazi salute at a rally in Nuremburg, Germany, in 1928. Bottom: By 1933, when the Nazis came to power, their anti-Semitic campaign included boycotts of businesses owned by Jews. In this photo, a Nazi stormtrooper stands beside a business vandalized with a painted Jewish Star of David and a sign reading, "Germans! Defend yourselves! Do not buy from Jews!"*

Elsa would be in danger if they ever went back to Berlin.

In the spring of 1933, when Albert and Elsa were still in Pasadena, the Gestapo—the brutal German secret police—ransacked the couple's Berlin apartment. Elsa's daughters, who still lived there, were terrified. Fortunately, the sisters had the foresight to smuggle all of Albert's important papers to the French embassy. The Gestapo found nothing. Next, they raided Albert and Elsa's country home, just outside Berlin, again finding nothing of importance.

The Nazis further stepped up their attack on Albert, putting his name at the top of a list of "enemies of the state." They offered a reward for his capture, seized all his property, and froze his bank accounts, so he could not get to his money in Germany. On top of that, they made a public event out of burning Albert's books, along with those written by other Jews and writers whose work they hated.

## RY TO A SCIENCE SUPERSTAR

whirlwind lifestyle finally caught up with him. One day, he Doctors diagnosed him with severe heart trouble, and it before he recovered. His wife Elsa could no longer handle all ed on her. Managing the house, dealing with Albert's masses e, and becoming his nurse were just too much. Albert hired Dukas, who was also a German Jew. When the Einsteins ted States, she went with them. She worked with Albert for rs, staying with him until the day he died.

That summer, Albert and Elsa spent two months in Belgium, under the protection of the Belgian Royal Family. Still, the danger was too great in Europe for the wanted man and his wife. They moved on, briefly visiting Britain, where a posse of armed guards safeguarded them. It was clear the couple could not return to Germany. In fact, Albert and Elsa never set foot in their homeland again.

Instead, in October 1933, they moved to New Jersey, where Albert had been offered a job at the new Institute of Advanced Study at Princeton University. The Institute had opened in 1930 as a place where leading scientists could conduct research undisturbed.

Albert's German secretary Helen Dukas moved to Princeton with the Einsteins and, a year later, Elsa's daughter Margot joined them there, too. She had moved to the safety of Paris with her sister Ilse but, when Ilse died of cancer in June 1934, Margot moved to the United States.

*"Living with Professor Einstein, I was accustomed to things turning into a circus wherever he went."*

Helen Dukas, Albert's longtime secretary

## Princeton = Peace + Quiet

Albert, Elsa, Margot, and Helen easily settled into a modest life in New Jersey. At first, Albert was mobbed everywhere he went. Before long, though, people got used to seeing the celebrity scientist in the neighborhood and they stopped fussing over him every time he strolled by.

Albert enjoyed the peace of the Institute, which he called a "free thinker's paradise." Tucked away in his office, away from the main university campus and Princeton's busy

## ELEMENTS OF EINSTEIN

Albert once said of his love for music, "If I were not a physicist, I would probably be a musician. I often think in music."

# CITIZEN EINSTEIN

Albert Einstein gave up his German citizenship at age 16, taking Swiss citizenship five years later. He had no intention of ever becoming a German citizen again. In fact, he only agreed to work at the University of Berlin, beginning in 1914, if there were "no change of my nationality," meaning he would be allowed to remain a Swiss citizen. The Kaiser, or Emperor, approved this condition. Even when Albert swore allegiance in his native land following World War I, he did not become a German citizen.

Fast forward to 1922, when Albert was (belatedly) awarded the 1921 Nobel Prize in Physics. At the time of the ceremony, he was in Asia and unable to attend. That meant the ambassador of his country had to accept the prize in his absence. In a bit of confusion, the German ambassador accepted the award on Albert's behalf before realizing that Albert was not a German citizen. As soon as Albert returned from Asia, the German government tried to cover this mistake by telling him that he had, in fact, taken German citizenship in 1919.

Albert decided not to cause a fuss, and he became a German citizen once again—but kept his Swiss citizenship. When he left Germany for the last time in 1933, he began the process of renouncing his unwanted German citizenship for the second time. By this time, though, the new Nazi government in Germany had declared Albert an "enemy of the state." Rather than allowing him to give up his citizenship, the Nazis made a public show of kicking him out of the country a year later. On March 29, 1934, Albert Einstein's German citizenship, which he never actually claimed, was revoked, or withdrawn.

*"If my theory of relativity is proven successful, Germany will claim me as a German and France will declare that I am a citizen of the world. Should my theory prove untrue, France will say that I am a German and Germany will declare that I am a Jew."*

Albert Einstein, speaking before a group of university professors in France, 1922

streets, Albert could focus all his attention on physics. He walked to and from work every day, stopping to chat or play with children along the way. One child famously asked Albert why he never wore socks. "I've reached an age where, if somebody tells me to wear socks, I don't have to," he replied.

When he wasn't working, Albert could be found riding his bicycle, sailing, and entertaining guests from all over the world. One of his greatest pleasures throughout his life was playing his violin. He played to help him relax and solve problems, and he played to entertain his friends. "I live my daydreams in music," he once said. "I see my life in terms of music. I get most joy in life out of music."

## ELEMENTS OF EINSTEIN

When Albert first arrived at the Institute of Advanced Study at Princeton, his new colleagues asked what equipment he needed for his new office. He replied: "A desk or table, a chair, paper, and a pencil. Oh, yes, and a large wastebasket, so I can throw away my mistakes."

Albert's life wasn't exactly ordinary, though. He and Elsa once traveled to Washington, DC, to have dinner with President and Mrs. Roosevelt. They stayed overnight at the White House.

Sadly, Elsa Einstein died in December 1936 of heart and kidney disease. Helen Dukas had always looked after Albert's schedule and correspondence, and protected him from what she called "the curious, the reporters, and the crazies." Following Elsa's death, Helen also became his housekeeper. Three years later, Albert's sister Maja moved to Princeton to live with her brother. Maja had been living

in Florence, Italy, but when the Italian government began to join forces with Nazi Germany, she knew she had to get out of Italy. Albert was thrilled to have his beloved sister by his side once again.

Now that he was settled into life in America, Albert joined social justice movements and criticized the growing gap between rich and poor people in the United States. He tackled rising anti-Semitism among students at Princeton, and became involved in a number of other important causes. Albert's activism made some of his colleagues at the Institute uncomfortable, but that never stopped him from speaking his mind.

By day, Albert continued to work on his unified field theory. He also debated physics with other scientists, most notably his friend and colleague Niels Bohr. At the time, most physicists agreed with Bohr that it is impossible to predict the behavior of a subatomic particle,

Albert Einstein's friend and colleague Niels Bohr (shown here with Albert in 1930) was awarded the 1922 Nobel Prize in Physics on the same day that the 1921 prize was belatedly given to Albert. Like Albert, Niels stood up against the Nazi Party before and during World War II. Niels, who was Jewish on his mother's side, helped many scientists escape from Germany into his own country, Denmark. When Germany invaded Denmark in 1943, Niels was forced to flee. Eventually, he settled in the United States, where he helped develop the atomic bomb.

## EINSTEIN'S ELUSIVE THEORY

Albert Einstein spent the last 30 years of his life unsuccessfully trying to formulate a theory that would explain the nature and behavior of all ma in the universe. Even though other scientists thought Albert was wastin his time, he persisted in seeking his unified field theory. He believed th fields of electromagnetics, gravity, space, and time could be connected predicted—by a single equation. Today, scientists continue to search for "theory of everything," which is similar to (but even a bit more complica than) Albert's unified field theory. So far, nobody has been able to form this theory, which one scientist called "an equation an inch long that wc allow us to read the mind of God."

such as an electron. That means the electron moves in random ways within an atom. Albert didn't like things that couldn't be predicted or measured. He didn't believe anything was random. "God does not play dice with the universe," he said. In this case, Albert was

# EINSTEIN THE INVENTOR

Albert Einstein was best known for his work in physics, but he was also an inventor. During his life, he worked with other inventors and scientists to create and patent a number of devices. In 1926, he and one of his former students were granted their first patent for a "noiseless" refrigerator that didn't require electricity. Over the next seven years, the duo would be granted a total of 45 patents related to this project. In 1934, Albert teamed up with an engineer to develop and patent a type of hearing aid. In 1935, he and a colleague patented an automatic camera that could focus and set the appropriate light level by itself. In 1936, Albert was granted what might be his oddest patent—for a blouse with "side openings … which also serve as arm holes."

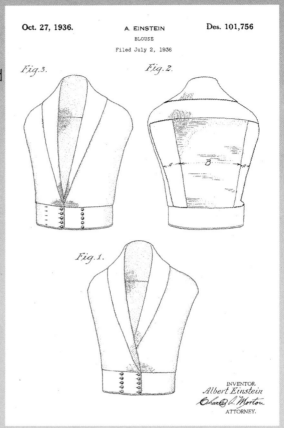

Oct. 27, 1936.   A. EINSTEIN   Des. 101,756
BLOUSE
Filed July 2, 1936

Fig.3.   Fig.2.

Fig.1.

INVENTOR.
Albert Einstein
Charles A. Morton
ATTORNEY.

wrong, but his objections and questions pushed physicists to refine their understanding of quantum theory, which is central to physics today.

## Meanwhile, Back in Germany …

As he worked away in peaceful Princeton, Albert could not ignore what was happening in his homeland. He continued to speak out against Nazism. He cut his ties with the scientific community in Germany, which supported the Nazis. He helped refugees, especially Jews, flee from the growing tyranny in Europe.

At this time, Albert faced a great dilemma. Since his youth, he had been a pacifist, opposing war and the use of military might to solve the world's problems. He realized the Nazis had to be stopped, and the only way to do that was for the rest of the world to stand strong against them. Eventually, he went against his own pacifist views. As he wrote to an American university student:

> *"Organized power can be opposed only by organized power. Much as I regret this, there is no other way."*

*Albert Einstein is met at the airport in Newark, New Jersey, in 1939. Even from a considerable distance, Albert is easy to spot in a group!*

In 1939, with that conclusion now existing alongside his longstanding pacifist beliefs, Albert wrote to U.S. president Franklin D. Roosevelt, suggesting that the United States develop an atomic bomb. He had heard that the Germans might be building such a bomb, and wanted to make sure the Americans beat them to it. He would later say that writing this letter was "the greatest mistake of my life." Historians still argue about whether Albert's letter influenced the president to order scientists to develop the bomb.

One month later, on September 1, 1939, Germany invaded Poland. World War II in Europe had begun.

On December 7, 1941, Germany's wartime partner Japan bombed Pearl

# CODE NAME: MANHATTAN

The Manhattan Project was a secret mission by the U.S. government to build an atomic bomb before Nazi Germany did. It was named after the island of Manhattan in New York City, where some of the research was conducted. During earlier phases of the project, it had been known by different code names. "Manhattan" was the construction phase. The project, which began in 1942, was centered in the desert in New Mexico, where tests could be conducted in secret. The project was so secret that many of the people working on it in labs and workshops around the country didn't even know what they were working on! The project created two atomic bombs that were dropped on Japan in August 1945, ending World War II.

Albert Einstein's letter to President Roosevelt may have prompted the U.S. government to begin research work on the atomic bomb, but Albert was never directly involved in the project. First of all, some government officials were suspicious of him, given his history and his outspokenness. They didn't trust him with such a huge American secret. Secondly, nuclear engineering was not Albert's area of expertise.

Harbor, Hawaii, bringing the United States into World War II. The U.S. government had ordered scientists to begin researching the atomic bomb well before Japan attacked Pearl Harbor. It would not be until 1942, however, that the government, with help from Canada and Britain, launched the "Manhattan Project" to actually build one. Albert was not directly involved with this project, even though his famous equation $E = mc^2$ was at the core of it. The equation allowed scientists to figure out how much power an atomic bomb would release.

In 1945, after Albert realized just how devastating the atomic bomb might be, he wrote a second letter to President Roosevelt,

*These photos show the mushroom clouds created by atomic bombs dropped on Hiroshima (left) and Nagasaki (right), Japan, as they rise miles (kilometers) above the cities in August 1945. The bombs ended World War II, but Albert Einstein was so horrified by the destruction caused by atomic bombs that he spent the rest of his life speaking out against nuclear war.*

urging him not to use the bomb. The president died before he read the letter. On August 6, 1945, acting under orders of President Harry S. Truman, the United States dropped an atomic bomb on Hiroshima, Japan. Three days later, it dropped a second one on Nagasaki. About 200,000 people were killed or injured in these attacks. Japan immediately surrendered, ending World War II.

## After the War

In 1945, the year World War II ended, Albert was 66 years old and suffering from heart and stomach ailments. He officially retired from Princeton University that year, but he continued to go to his office a few days a week. He never stopped working on his unified field theory, and he never managed to completely figure it out.

Despite his passion for physics, Albert refused to reconnect with scientists in Germany.

# THE WORLD AT WAR

World War II began on September 1, 1939, when the military forces of Nazi Germany invaded Poland. Within days, Poland, Britain, France, Canada, Australia, New Zealand, India, and South Africa declared war on Germany.

During the six years of World War II, almost every country in the world became involved in the conflict. If a country sided with Germany, it was part of the so-called "Axis." If it sided with Britain and France, it was one of the "Allies."

In Europe, Nazi Germany took over countries in all directions. By 1943, the Nazis had increased their territory to include most of continental Europe as we know it today. They made a big mistake, though, when they invaded the Soviet Union in 1941.

At that point, the Soviet Union joined the Allies in fighting against Germany, greatly increasing the number of forces opposing the Nazis. Later that same year, Japan, which sided with Germany, bombed Pearl Harbor, Hawaii. That brought the United States into the war.

With so much international might dedicated to overthrowing the Axis, Germany surrendered on May 7, 1945. This ended the war in Europe. The war in Asia ended four months later, after the United States dropped two atomic bombs on Japan. More than 120,000 civilians, or non-military people, died because of those bombs—either during the bombings or from radiation exposure after the bombings. Japan quickly surrendered.

World War II was the biggest war in history. About 100 million military personnel fought in the war, and 50 to 70 million civilians died, making it the deadliest war in history. It was also the only war in which nuclear weapons were used.

He was horrified at what his homeland had done—to the rest of the world, and to Jewish people in particular—during World War II. By the time the war ended, the Nazis had killed 6 million Jews and millions of other European civilians, including women and children. "The Germans have slaughtered my Jewish brethren," said Albert. "I will have nothing further to do with the Germans."

# Europe's Darkest Days

During World War II, the Nazis murdered 6 million Jews, along with millions of others. Most of the victims, especially the Jews, were targeted as being racially or ethnically "inferior" to the Nazis' vision of a "master race" made up of people of northern European descent. Jews were rounded up and packed into crowded disease-ridden ghettos. There, most of those who did not die of disease and starvation were crammed into railroad cattle cars and shipped to concentration camps. Most died in these camps. There, along with other victims of the Nazis, they were shot by firing squads, or worked or starved to death. In the case of the Jews, many were also killed in massive gas chambers. Many years after the war, this organized government-authorized slaughter became known by the term "Holocaust," a word of Greek origin meaning "sacrifice by fire."

*By the 1940s, the Nazis' persecution of Jews and others in Germany and other parts of Europe had reached the level of genocide, or mass killings to exterminate an entire people. This photo, one of the most dramatic to come out of World War II, was taken in 1943. It shows German soldiers rounding up men, women, and children for deportation and death following a failed Jewish uprising in the Warsaw Ghetto, in Poland.*

For the rest of his life, Albert used his fame to lobby for equal rights for minorities, and to promote world peace and international cooperation. He supported the budding civil rights movement in the United States. He was pro-civil liberties and anti-poverty. He even said that the United States and the Soviet Union should work together to make sure nuclear war never happened. This position shocked many Americans who, in the years after World War II, had become accustomed to viewing the Soviet Union as the greatest threat to the United States.

As Albert aged, he traveled less frequently, and his time became more and more consumed with replying to fan mail. Thousands of people, including many children, wrote to the person known to many as "the world's smartest man," seeking his wisdom and advice.

But the great scientist was definitely slowing down. His health was declining and, in the years following the death of his wife Elsa in 1936, other loved ones were passing on. His first wife Mileva died after a stroke in 1948, and his beloved sister Maja died in 1951, when Albert was 72.

Despite his ill health, his sadness over losing Maja, and the feeling that he was out of the loop when it came to the latest scientific research, Albert refused to stop working. Several times a week, rain or shine, he walked to his office at the Institute of Advanced Study, to exercise his great brain.

# Chapter 6
# Einstein = "Genius"

By 1951, Albert Einstein, now in his 70s, was no longer traveling the world—partly because of his failing health, and partly because he was tired of the celebrity spotlight. In a letter to a friend that year, he wrote: "Because of a peculiar popularity which I have acquired, anything I do is likely to develop into a ridiculous comedy. This means that I have to stay close to my home and rarely leave Princeton." But that didn't mean he was no longer working. Later in the same letter, he told his friend: "What has remained [for me] is the relentless work on difficult scientific problems. The fascinating magic of that work will continue to my last breath."

*A photo of Albert Einstein taken around 1947, when he was about 68 years old.*

## Trying Times

True to his word, Albert Einstein spent the last few years of his life working on his unified field theory, which he called "one simple theory that could explain all the laws of physics." At the same time, he used his enduring fame to draw attention to causes he cared about. He lobbied against nuclear war and promoted world peace. He was a great supporter of the growing civil rights movement in the United States. He spoke out against U.S. senator Joseph McCarthy and his famous anti-communist crusade.

As much as Albert loved his adopted homeland, he could not remain silent while citizens were labeled "un-American," and their lives and careers ruined, over their political beliefs. He felt McCarthy's actions threatened intellectual freedom and democracy itself. "The current investigations are...[a] greater danger to

# THE FBI FILE

From the time Albert Einstein moved to the United States to the day he died, the FBI, or Federal Bureau of Investigation, kept a secret file on him. Albert was a pacifist and a liberal thinker who believed in freedom of speech and equality for all. As such, he was considered by some to be a threat to the United States. He was associated with a number of organizations the government found objectionable, and he spoke up for civil rights, social justice, and other causes he believed in.

During the so-called Red Scare of the 1950s, he became even more outspoken. The only thing that saved Albert from being on Senator Joseph McCarthy's "black list" and facing persecution was his fame. Nobody, even the U.S. government, dared attack the beloved absent-minded professor. In the end, the FBI's Einstein file contained more than 1,800 pages of documents, rumors, and guesswork.

# McCarthyism

After World War II ended, communism was on the rise in some nations throughout the world. These included China and many Eastern European nations under the influence of the Soviet Union, whose government had long been led by the Communist Party.

Communism is built on the belief that everyone in a community should share everything equally, so nobody has more than anyone else. In practice, communist states often put into effect harsh laws to uphold their beliefs. The U.S. government portrayed communism as a threat to the American way of life. From 1948 until about 1956, the government actively targeted members of the Communist Party and their associates. The goal was to restrict or eliminate certain belief systems that disagreed with that of the government, and to rid the nation of these so-called "un-American" people. During this time, called the Red Scare because red was a color identified with communism, people from all walks of life were harassed.

Beginning in 1950, U.S. senator Joseph McCarthy, a Republican from Wisconsin, made it his business to "save" Americans from communist spies. He held hearings, intimidated people, threatened them with prison, and ruined their careers and reputations in his efforts to get information. In most cases, the senator had no evidence to support his attacks on innocent people. In the end, nobody on McCarthy's hit list was ever convicted of subversion, or undermining the government.

Eventually, Americans realized McCarthy's actions were wrong, and the government put a stop to his attacks. His tactics led to a 1957 U.S. Supreme Court ruling that now protects the rights of witnesses.

The term "McCarthyism" has come to refer to any process of targeted, false accusation, fueled by mass hysteria or fear.

*U.S. Senator Joseph McCarthy in 1954, at the time he held hearings aimed at exposing supposed communists in the U.S. Army.*

## ELEMENTS OF EINSTEIN

In his last years, Albert Einstein stopped playing his beloved violin. "I am done with fiddling," he wrote to a friend in 1951. "With the passage of years, it has become more and more unbearable for me to listen to my own playing."

our society than those few Communists in our country could ever be," said Albert, one of the first people to speak up against McCarthy and his so-called "witch-hunt." Some politicians believed Albert was a threat to the United States. The whole time he lived in America, the FBI kept an eye on him, documenting his activities in a thick file.

## President Einstein?

Meanwhile, the government of Israel offered Albert its ultimate honor. Throughout his life, Albert's connection and commitment to the international Jewish community had continued to strengthen. Because of that bond, and because he was considered the world's most famous and brilliant Jewish person, he was asked to become the second-ever president of the newly formed Jewish nation of Israel.

*Albert Einstein and Israeli Prime Minister David Ben-Gurion share a light moment at Albert's home in Princeton, New Jersey, in 1951. This was about a year before Ben-Gurion offered Albert—and Albert declined— the position of president of the recently created State of Israel.*

In Israel, the prime minister is the elected leader of the government, and the president mostly represents the nation at official state functions. Still, Albert would have brought great fame and respect to the new country and to the position. His friend Chaim Weizmann had been the nation's president since its founding in 1948. After Weizmann died in 1952, Prime Minister David Ben-Gurion turned to Albert, who declined the offer. "I am deeply moved by the offer ... and at once saddened and ashamed that I cannot accept it," he said.

As a man of science, he said he lacked "both a natural aptitude and the experience to deal properly with people and, exercise official functions. For these reasons alone, I should be unsuited to fulfill the duties of that high office, even if advancing age was not making increasing inroads on my strength." By this time, the great scientist was a 73-year-old in ill health—and he wanted to reserve what time he had left for physics.

That time ran out three years later. On April 13, 1955, Albert suffered an aneurism in the form of a burst blood vessel in his stomach. He spent the next five days in the hospital, where he never stopped working. He continued to

## THE LAST WORDS OF ALBERT EINSTEIN

Just before he died, Albert Einstein uttered a few words in German. The only person in the room was a nurse who did not speak German, so the scientist's last words will never be known. In his notebook at his bedside were 12 pages of calculations, and a draft of a radio speech he was scheduled to deliver on Israeli Independence Day a few weeks later.

make notes and work on calculations related to his unified field theory right to his last day. The great physicist died just after 1:00 A.M. on April 18, 1955, with his notebooks at his side. Wrote his stepdaughter Margot,

*"As fearless as he had been all his life, so he faced death humbly and quietly. He left the world without sentimentality or regrets."*

News of Albert's death made headlines, dominating the front pages of newspapers all over the world.

At his request, there was no funeral, and there is no marked grave. His body was cremated, and his ashes scattered in a location that remains secret to this day. He requested that his house in Princeton not be turned into a museum (a wish that has been honored), and that his brain be studied to find the secret to his brilliance.

# THE GREAT BRAIN

When Albert Einstein died, his brain was removed, preserved, photographed, and cut up into 240 chunks to allow scientists all over the world to have a look. Their goal? To determine whether the brain of the genius physicist was any different than a "normal" brain. Some scientists have declared that Albert's brain was "very different," or smaller, or more complex than normal, or missing a particular structure. Others have said the research proves nothing. "We're dealing with just one brain and this makes it impossible to draw any firm conclusions about the population at large," said a Welsh neuroscientist. "Human brains come in all shapes and sizes and there is no known relationship to cognition [thought]. Very few people have the 'normal' brain we see in textbooks, and neither did Einstein."

In his will, Albert left his violin to his grandson, and all his papers to Hebrew University in Jerusalem, Israel.

## Albert Einstein Lives On

Albert Einstein made sure nobody could "worship my bones" at a gravesite, but there was no way he could halt the tributes paid to him since his passing. In 1955, a newly discovered element in the Periodic Table—Einsteinium—was named for him. That same year, a crater on the Moon was renamed "Einstein" and, in 1956, Israel dedicated a postage stamp to the great physicist, as have dozens of other nations since then. In 1973, astronomers who discovered a new asteroid near Mars named it "2001 Einstein." In 1979, celebrations, conferences, and events around the world honored the 100th anniversary of his birth.

In its last issue of the 20th century, a century "that will be remembered foremost for its science and technology," *Time* magazine named Albert Einstein "Person of the Century."

*In 1968, the Bank of Israel began featuring Albert Einstein's picture on the nation's 5 lirot bill.*

In that issue, published on December 31, 1999, writer Frederic Golden described Albert in the following way:

*"... the embodiment of pure intellect, the bumbling professor with the German accent.... Yet he was unfathomably profound—the genius among geniuses who discovered, merely by thinking about it, that the universe was not as it seemed."*

# ODES TO EINSTEIN

As Albert insisted, his former home in Princeton remains a private residence, rather than a museum. Still, people from around the world regularly visit the house (shown here) just to see where the legendary physicist spent the last 20 years of his life. The house was designated a National Historic Landmark in 1979. The town of Princeton erected a monument to Albert in 2005 and, at Caltech, where Albert once taught, is a small sculpture of Albert playing the violin. Of all the Einstein sculptures around the world—and there are many—the most famous, and likely the largest, is the huge Einstein Memorial located at the National Academy of Sciences in Washington, DC, (shown below). Like many depictions of the great physicist, it captures the essence of a man whose casual, often rumpled, manner endeared him to generations of ordinary people all over the globe.

Five years later, the United Nations declared 2005 the "World Year of Physics," in honor of the 100th anniversary of Albert's *annus mirabilis*, or "miracle year." That was 1905, the year he penned his special theory of relativity. Around the world, people celebrated Albert's genius with commemorations, lectures, and special events dedicated to the great scientist. In Waterloo, Ontario, just outside Toronto, more than 28,000 people attended a month-long EinsteinFest. In the United Kingdom, citizens celebrated what they called "Einstein Year" with new plays, dance performances, and movies about Albert's life. The UK celebration also included community events, special projects, and even an actor playing a "surfing Albert Einstein" who spoke about the physics of hanging ten and other surfing maneuvers.

*The popular image of Albert Einstein sticking out his tongue has been turned into a frothy design sitting atop a cup of coffee.*

# ELEMENTS OF EINSTEIN

Just because Albert Einstein was a public figure, it doesn't mean just anyone can use his name. The name "Einstein" is actually a licensed trademark owned by Hebrew University in Jerusalem. That means you have to have the university's permission (and pay a fee) before you use his picture or name anything—a TV show, building, street, or toy—after the famous physicist. The university earns about a million dollars a year on royalties from such projects and products.

Since his death about 60 years ago, Albert has been the subject of countless books, films, and theater projects. There have been "Baby Einstein" toys, a kids' cartoon series called *Little Einsteins*, an Australian TV game show called *The Einstein Factor*, a video game character named Professor Albert Einstein, and even an opera called *Einstein on the Beach*. Facebook and Twitter feature multiple pages in Albert's honor and, all over the world, schools, buildings, and streets are named for him.

Albert's image adorns T-shirts, mugs, calendars, buttons, and bookmarks. There are Einstein stuffed toys, puppets, bobble-heads, jigsaw puzzles, mouse pads, computer thumb drives, bookends, wallets, and even underpants. You name it, there is an Einstein version of it!

## Albert Einstein's Greatest Legacy

While the image of the shaggy-haired genius has become a pop culture icon, Albert Einstein's greatest legacy is felt in the world of physics. "The scientific touchstones [significant achievements] of our age—the bomb, space travel, electronics—all bear his fingerprints," wrote James Gleick in a 1999 special edition of *Time* magazine dedicated to 20th century scientists. "He discovered, just by thinking about it, the essential structure of the cosmos."

It's true. Albert's discoveries have led to everything from nuclear power to TV remote controls, laser surgery to CD players, x-rays to GPS—the worldwide system for finding exact locations. While we don't necessarily understand his theories, we know he revolutionized our lives.

# Children of Genius

Albert Einstein had two sons with his first wife Mileva Maric, and two stepdaughters, who were the children of his second wife Elsa Einstein.

When Albert and Mileva split up, the boys stayed with their mother in Zurich, Switzerland. The oldest, Hans Albert, eventually earned a graduate degree from the Zurich Polytechnic—the school his father had attended. Like his father, he married a woman his parents—at least his father—did not care for. Fortunately for Hans Albert, his marriage was a happy one. He and his wife had four sons, three of whom died in childhood, and an adopted daughter. In 1938, Hans Albert moved his family to the United States. He became a professor at the University of California, Berkeley, and saw his father often. Hans Albert died of heart failure in 1973, at the age of 69.

Albert's younger son Eduard lived a less happy life. An excellent student who loved literature and music, he studied medicine in the hopes of becoming a psychiatrist. Unfortunately, Eduard suffered from mental illness that forced him to quit school. He spent much of his life in a psychiatric hospital in Zurich, and he last saw his father in 1933. Eduard died in 1965, at the age of 55, following a stroke.

Albert's eldest stepdaughter Ilse, was 21 when Albert married her mother. Always interested in politics, arts, and literature, Ilse married a magazine editor, with whom she escaped to Holland from pre-World War II Nazi Germany. Later, she moved to Paris, where she died of cancer in 1934, at the age of 36.

Margot, Albert's younger stepdaughter, married a Russian writer with whom she moved to Paris. When the couple split up, Margot moved to the United States to live with her mother and stepfather. After Albert's death, Margot continued to live in the Einstein's Princeton home with Albert's secretary Helen Dukas, who died in 1982. Margot died in 1986, at the age of 86.

*Albert Einstein and son Hans Albert Einstein (right) greet one another at the airport in New York in 1937. Taking his father's advice, Hans Albert moved his family from Switzerland to the United States before the Nazi threat in Europe grew more dangerous than it had already become.*

*This photo, taken in 1920, shows Albert in the Netherlands visiting his friend and fellow physicist Paul Ehrenfest. Ehrenfest's son, Paul Jr., sits on Albert's lap. The photo captures several facets of the life and personality of Albert Einstein—his devotion to physics, the fellowship he shared with fellow European scientists before the outbreak of Nazism across the continent, and a special quality that appealed to adults and children alike.*

Even his name has become a part of our vocabulary—a noun used as another word for "genius." You might say, "He's no Einstein," when talking about someone who is not too smart. Or, "it doesn't take an Einstein" to figure out something simple. "In this busy [20th] century, dominated like no other by science ...

he stands alone as our emblem of intellectual power," wrote Gleick. "We talk as though humanity could be divided into two groups: Albert Einstein and everybody else."

It's not just this brilliance that keeps Albert Einstein alive in our society, though. Albert was a rare blend of scientific genius and quirky guy-next-door. His sense of childlike wonder and curiosity led him to transform our understanding of time, space, and the world around us. His charming eccentricities and commitment to making that world a better place made him a lovable symbol and hero for the ages.

He once said, in his typically humble way, "All I have tried to do in my life is to ask a few questions." Fortunately for the rest of us, Albert didn't give up until he found the answers to those questions—even if it took him 10 years to figure out what would happen if he could ride on a beam of light.

*A. Einstein.*

# Chronology

**March 14, 1879** Albert Einstein born in Ulm, Germany.

**1880** Family moves to Munich.

**1881** Sister Maria, or "Maja," born.

**1885** Albert starts school.

**1888** Accepted into more competitive Luitpold-Gymnasium, designed to prepare students for university.

**1894** After father's business fails, family moves to Italy, Albert continues studies in Munich; later leaves Munich to join family in Italy.

**1895** Takes, and fails, entrance exams to gain admission to Swiss Federal Polytechnic in Zurich, Switzerland.

**1895–1896** Spends year at a high school in Aarau, Switzerland; there, conducts first "thought experiment."

**1896** Renounces German citizenship; takes Polytechnic exams second time; is accepted; meets Mileva Maric, only female student in class.

**1900** Graduates from Polytechnic; Mileva fails to graduate.

**1901** Becomes Swiss citizen.

**1902** Albert and Mileva have daughter, Lieserl, out of wedlock; starts work as patent clerk in Bern; father Hermann dies.

**1903** Albert and Mileva marry.

**1904** First son Hans Albert born.

**1905** Albert's *annus mirabilis*; publishes four groundbreaking papers in German scientific journal, including Special Theory of Relativity and paper that introduces his famous equation $E = mc^2$; earns Ph.D. from University of Zurich.

**1908** Gets first teaching job, part-time at University of Bern.

**1909** Gets full-time teaching job at University of Zurich; quits patent job.

**1910** Second son Eduard born.

**1911** Family moves to Prague, Czechoslovakia; Albert takes job at German University; takes part in first Solvay Congress in Brussels, Belgium.

**1912** Moves family back to Zurich to start teaching at Zurich Polytechnic.

**1914** Moves family to Berlin, takes non-teaching job at University of Berlin; Mileva and Albert separate;

Mileva and sons move back to Zurich; World War I begins in Europe.

**1916** Publishes General Theory of Relativity.

**1918** World War I ends.

**1919** Albert and Mileva divorce; marries cousin Elsa; astronomers observe solar eclipse, proving General Theory of Relativity correct; becomes international celebrity.

**1920** Mother Pauline dies.

**1921** With Elsa, joins Zionist leaders on U.S. speaking tour; meets President Warren G. Harding; mobbed by fans everywhere he goes.

**1922** Awarded 1921 Nobel Prize in Physics.

**1928** Collapses from overexertion, diagnosed with heart trouble; hires a secretary, Helen Dukas, who will work for him for next 27 years.

**1930** First grandchild born; Albert and Elsa spend winter in Pasadena; becomes visiting professor at Caltech; spends next two winters there.

**1933** Hitler takes power in Germany; Gestapo ransacks Albert's two homes in Berlin; announces he will never return to Germany; moves to Princeton with Elsa and Helen; takes post at Princeton University.

**1934** Elsa's daughter Ilse dies in Paris; her other daughter Margot moves to Princeton.

**1936** Elsa Einstein dies.

**1939** Albert writes to U.S. president Franklin D. Roosevelt suggesting United States develop an atomic bomb; sister Maja moves to Princeton to live with him; World War II begins in Europe.

**1940** Albert, Margot, and Helen become U.S. citizens.

**1941** Japan attacks U.S. Navy Center in Pearl Harbor; United States enters World War II.

**1945** Writes second Roosevelt letter, urging him not to use atomic bomb; Roosevelt dies before reading letter; Germany surrenders, ending World War II in Europe; four months later, United States drops two atomic bombs on Japan, ending World War II in Pacific; retires from Princeton, but keeps office there for rest of life.

**1948** First wife Mileva dies.

**1951** Sister Maja dies.

**1952** Offered presidency of Israel, a ceremonial position he declines.

**April 18, 1955** Albert Einstein dies in Princeton, New Jersey.

# Glossary

**academia** The world of higher education; the culture and community of colleges and universities

**academic standing** Ranking in one's class at school

**atomic bomb** A bomb of enormous power; its explosive energy comes from a chemical reaction that involves splitting atoms

**bookish** Seriously studious; learning by reading and studying, rather than by life experience

**civil rights movement** An organized effort to stop discrimination against people of certain races; the civil rights movement in the United States (1954–1968) focused on the rights of African Americans

**computer chip** A tiny electronic circuit system that allows computers to store huge amounts of data

**doctorate degree** The highest academic degree a student can earn at a university

**electromagnetics** The branch of physics that deals with electrical charges, magnetic forces, and their interaction with each other; electromagnetic waves have characteristics of electricity and magnetism; when an electric charge moves, it creates a magnetic field; the combined effect is called electromagnetism

**electron** A tiny, negatively charged particle of energy in an atom

**embassy** A building where one country is represented in the capital city of another country

**engineering** A practical application of the physical sciences that deals with designing, planning, construction, and maintaining machinery, systems, or structures.

**ghetto** An area in a city where people of similar social, political, or economic backgrounds live together, usually in poor conditions

**honorary degree** A degree, usually a doctorate, given by a university to honor a person's achievements; the honoree does not have to complete usual requirements for the degree

**intellectual** A highly intelligent person who enjoys activities that involve thinking and figuring things out; usually refers to someone interested or involved in the arts or sciences

**manifesto** A public declaration of beliefs, opinion, or goals by an individual or group; sometimes includes a call for action or change

**multiple sclerosis (MS)** A chronic disease that affects the brain and spinal cord, often resulting in numbness, muscle weakness, vision problems, and difficulty balancing

**Periodic Table of the Elements** A table that shows all known chemical elements, or atoms, in order of atomic number, or the number of protons in the atom's nucleus

**philosophy** A school of thought that questions concepts such as truth, life, existence, and reality

**physicist** A scientist who researches subjects in physics

**physics** A branch of science dealing with matter, energy, force, and motion, and how they relate to each other

**progressive** Moving forward, exploring new ways of thinking, and supporting change, rather than wanting to keep things the way they are

**radioactivity** Also called "radioactive decay"; describes the spontaneous release of electrons from certain unstable elements, such as uranium. Energy is released during this process

**royalties** Money paid on every sale of a certain product to the person or company that created it

**scientific journal** A periodical for scientists that features articles about new developments in a particular branch of science

**solar eclipse** The Moon passing between Earth and the Sun, and fully or partially blocking the Sun

**stroke** A sudden blockage of blood flow to the brain, or the rupture of a blood vessel in the brain; often results in loss of mobility or speech; sometimes causes death

**symmetrical** Having sides or halves that are the same, mirror images of each other

**textile** Fabric; the textile industry involves making fabrics or using fabrics, fibers, and yarns to make other things, such as clothing

**theoretical physics** A branch of physics that uses equations, calculations, and other forms of math, rather than experimentation, to explain natural phenomena

**thesis** A lengthy academic research paper that a student writes as a condition of earning a graduate degree from a university

**trademark** A word, phrase, symbol, or name that is associated with a certain person or product and is legally protected; the trademark cannot be used by anyone else without permission of the owner

**tuition** A sum of money a student pays to a school to be permitted to attend classes there

**tyranny** Cruel, unreasonable, and unjust government, by a single person or a group

# Further Information

## Books

Brallier, Jess. *Who Was Albert Einstein?*
New York: Grosset & Dunlap, 2002.

Ferguson Delano, Marfé. *Genius: A Photobiography of Albert Einstein*.
Washington, DC: National Geographic Children's Books, 2008.

Isaacson, Walter. *Einstein: His Life and Universe*.
New York: Simon & Schuster, 2011.

MacLeod, Elizabeth. *Albert Einstein: A Life of Genius*.
Toronto: Kids Can Press, 2003.

Wishinsky, Frieda. *Albert Einstein: A Photographic Story of a Life*.
London/New York: Dorling Kindersley, 2005.

Yeatts, Tabatha. *Albert Einstein: The Miracle Mind*.
New York: Sterling Publishing, 2007.

## Video

*Einstein Revealed* (a PBS DVD/video). Green Umbrella, Ltd, for NOVA production.
First aired in 1997. Watch online: http://video.pbs.org/video/2035153862/

See also the homepage for *Einstein Revealed*: http://www.pbs.org/wgbh/nova/
physics/einstein-revealed.html#mep-related-links, which features a transcript of
the documentary and links to many excellent Einstein-related sites.

# Websites

**http://www.biography.com/people/albert-einstein-9285408**
This site presents a complete biography of Albert Einstein, divided into seven sections. It also includes a Quick Facts section, an excellent photo collection, and 11 short videos about Albert.

**http://www.amnh.org/exhibitions/past-exhibitions/einstein**
On this site, you can visit a virtual version of the American Museum of Natural History's exhibition about Albert Einstein. Titled simply "Einstein," the exhibition features biographical information about the great physicist. It also focuses on some of Albert's areas of interest—light, time, energy, gravity—and his non-scientific activities, such as his antinuclear-war activism.

**http://content.time.com/time/specials/packages/ article/0,28804,1936731_1936743,00.html**
This site, "20 Things You Need to Know About Einstein," is a sort of Q & A about Albert Einstein. It asks 20 questions about such things as Einstein's childhood, his Jewish faith, his theories, and his political beliefs. Each question comes with a short answer and a photo.

**http://www.physics4kids.com/index.html**
This site explains some basic principles of physics in a fairly simple way. It is divided into sections, including some on Albert Einstein's favorite subjects—motion, heat, and light. If you want to test your knowledge, take one of the quizzes on the site!

**http://einstein.biz/index.php**
This site has just a tiny biography of Albert Einstein, but what makes it worth visiting are the photo gallery and the page of quotes.

# Index

**a**bsent-mindedness
10, 12
*Annals of Physics*
*(Annalan der Physik)*
43, 50, 61
*Annus Mirabilis*
(Year of Wonders)
50, 54, 59
anti-Semitism 67, 74
antiwar views 25–27,
38, 59–60, 70, 83,
84, 92
appearance 9–11, 58
atomic bomb 75–76,
80, 81, 83, 87, 88
atoms 7, 46, 47, 48,
51, 84, 85–86, 87

**B**iedermeier ("nerd")
15, 22, 28
birthplace 17
Bohr, Niels 71, 80, 81
brain dissected 96
Brown, Robert 47
Brownian Motion
46–47

**C**alifornia Institute of
Technology (Caltech)
73, 98
cell phones 12, 48
childhood 12, 13,
15–18, 20, 33,
69

children
Eduard 58, 59, 64,
101
Hans Albert 41, 42,
59, 61, 65, 101
Lieserl 43
citizenships 8, 27, 38,
78, 84
communism 93
Curie, Irène 57
Curie, Marie 56, 57

**d**egrees
honorary 8, 54–55
Ph.D. 50
Dukas, Helen 76, 77,
79, 84, 101

**E** = mc2 6, 31, 50, 51,
54, 85
Einstein, Elsa, 65–66,
67, 68, 69, 71, 73,
74, 76, 77, 79
daughter Ilse 77, 101
daughter Margot 77,
84, 96, 101
Einstein, Hermann and
Pauline 16, 20, 24–25,
27, 31, 37–38, 41
Einstein, Maria (Maja)
15, 16, 18, 43,
79–80, 89
Einsteinhaus
(Einstein House) 42
electricity 7, 44, 46, 82

**f**ame 11, 26, 67–68,
70, 73, 77, 91, 92,
96,
name use 99–100
FBI file 92, 94

**g**eneral theory of
relativity 35, 61, 63,
64, 66
genius 9, 10, 24, 53,
98, 99, 101, 102,
103
Germany
anti-Semitism in 67,
75
Munich 15, 21,
24–25, 68
parents' home in 17
University of Berlin
53, 58, 78
in World War I
59–60, 64, 67
in World War II
4–78, 80, 81,
82–88, 101
gravesite 96, 97
Grossmann, Marcel
34, 35, 40, 61

**h**eart trouble 76, 101
Hitler, Adolf 74, 75
honors, posthumous
97–99
humanitarianism 12

Institute of Advanced
   Study 5, 79, 89
Israel 67, 68, 94,
   95, 97
Italy 22, 24–25, 80

Japan in WWII 84, 85,
   86, 87
Judaism 20, 69, 74

lasers 12, 45, 46, 100
light 5, 6, 7, 29, 42, 44,
   46, 48, 49, 61, 62,
   63, 64, 82
   beam puzzle 6, 29,
      41, 49, 101
   nature of 5–6, 41,
      49, 61–63
   speed of 7, 29, 44,
      49, 51
   structure of 44, 45,
      61

magnetism 7, 44
Manhattan Project 85
"Manifesto to
   Europeans" 60
Maric, Mileva 36–38,
   39, 41, 42, 43, 55,
   58, 59, 65, 66, 71
mathematics 12,
   21–24, 26, 35,
   36, 44, 57
   music and 18–19
McCarthy, Joseph
   92–94
military service 25,
   38–39
music, love of 18, 19,

29, 37, 77, 97
myths about 26,
   33, 71

Nobel Prize in Physics
   8, 50, 70–71, 73,
   74, 78, 81
   Marie Curie 57
   Niels Bohr 71, 81
   nominations for 55,
      58, 59, 71
nuclear power 48, 51,
   100

patent office 31,
   39–41, 53, 54, 60
patents held 40, 82
Periodic Table of the
   Elements 48, 97
"Person of the Century"
   13
photoelectric effect
   45, 46, 48, 71
photons 45, 46
photovoltaic cell 46
physics 5, 6, 8, 36, 43,
   71, 80, 86, 95, 102
   Einstein's study of
      26, 29, 32, 35
   electromagnetic
      waves 44, 46
   electromagnetics
      73, 81
   energy 7, 41, 44,
      45, 51
   gravity 44, 60, 61,
      62, 63
   laws and principles
      of 7, 44, 92

mass 49, 51
molecules 7,
   46–47, 48, 51
motion 7, 41, 42, 60
quantum 44, 45–46,
   48, 82
space 7, 23, 49, 73,
   81, 103
teaching of 53–54,
   58
theoretical 7, 71
time 7, 23, 42, 49,
   73, 81, 103
world of 6, 43, 44,
   50, 53, 100
Planck, Max 42, 44,
   53, 56

relativity 9, 55, 60–64,
   71, 78, 84, 99
   general theory of 6,
      7, 35, 61, 63,
      64, 66
   principles of 47,
      49–50

school
   dislike for 20, 21,
      22, 32, 34–35
   favorite subjects
      22–24, 26
   in Switzerland 5,
      27–29, 31, 32, 34
solar cells 46
Solvay Conference 56
Soviet Union 28, 87,
   89, 93

space, outer 12, 48, 49, 100
Big Bang theory 12
Sun 61, 62, 63
universe 12, 13, 19, 20, 48, 53, 64, 81, 98
Switzerland 101
education in 5, 26–28, 31–32, 34–35, 36
home in 42
military service in 38–39
patent office 31, 39–41, 53, 54, 60
teaching in 54, 58

Talmud, Max 23, 24, 68

thought experiments 5–6, 7, 12, 29, 41, 53, 60–61
*Time* magazine 13, 97, 100
trademarked name 99, 100

unified field theory 73, 80, 81, 86, 92, 96
United States 66, 83
citizenship 84
civil rights in 80, 89, 92
move to 73–74, 75, 76, 77, 101
Princeton home 96, 98, 101
Princeton University 5, 77, 79, 80,

86, 89
visits to 67, 68, 70, 73
in World War II 84–86, 87

Weizmann, Chaim 67, 68, 69, 95
World Year of Physics 99

x-rays 12, 100

Zionism 67, 70

# About the Author

Diane Dakers was born and raised in Toronto, and now makes her home in Victoria, British Columbia. Like Albert Einstein, Diane studied math and physics at university (along with chemistry). Unlike Albert, she switched careers and has been a newspaper, magazine, television, and radio journalist—specializing in arts and cultural issues—since 1991.